Applying UML

Applying UML:

Advanced Application

Rob Pooley
Pauline Wilcox

ELSEVIER
BUTTERWORTH
HEINEMANN

AMSTERDAM BOSTON HEIDELBERG LONDON NEW YORK OXFORD
PARIS SAN DIEGO SAN FRANCISCO SINGAPORE SYDNEY TOKYO

Butterworth-Heinemann is an imprint of Elsevier

Elsevier Butterworth-Heinemann
Linacre House, Jordan Hill, Oxford OX2 8DP
200 Wheeler Road, Burlington, MA 01803

First published 2004

British Library Cataloguing in Publication Data
A catalogue record for this book is available from the British Library

ISBN   0 7506 56832

For information on all Butterworth-Heinemann publications
visit our website at www.bh.com

Printed and bound in Great Britain

Contents

Preface

So why did we write "yet another" book on the UML? Does the world need it and what, if anything, makes it distinctive? The real answer is that the only way to answer those questions is to read the end result. Here, however, are some of our answers.

In an attempt to end the "object oriented Tower of Babel", the Unified Modelling Language (UML) has been adopted as a standard modelling notation by the Object Management Group (OMG). This book concerns itself with the application of the UML. There are numerous textbooks that discuss the UML notation or its use with regard to particular application domains, but all of these seem to us to focus on software engineering. Whilst the origins of the UML lie in the concerns of software engineering, it is steadily gaining acceptance in sometimes more diverse and sometimes more specific domains. For example, the UML is being considered increasingly as a notation to support business process modelling, in wide ranging ways, but it is also being applied to specific software engineering domains, such as real-time software development.

This book specifically uses UML 1.5, though some discussion is included about the probable impact of UML 2.0. Whichever version is taken, the impact on what we are trying to achieve is minimal.

The real motivation for this book is to provide a text that addresses the practical issues faced by people in adopting the UML. This is reflected in the suggested book title, the aim being to assist the reader *applying* UML rather than just *learning* the UML. Our aim is to illustrate how the notation can be applied across a broad range of problems, from business modelling through to software development. We, therefore, consider the impact of issues beyond the notation itself, specifically the adoption of a particular process or methodology. In general we find no convincing case for a specific choice in this area, preferring to base choices on the needs of the situation being modelled.

Who should read this book?

This book is intended for a wide range of readers, in both academia and industry. It is expected that the target reader will have some basic knowledge of modelling notations and the modelling activity, but is perhaps a little foggy about how the UML fits into the picture. They may perhaps have some knowledge of the UML notation, but be unclear how to tackle a given problem using it. This book tries to help you start to fill that gap, by examining the strengths and weaknesses of the notation and taking a practical and pragmatic approach to modelling. The book also has a role for the more experienced modeller in providing an opportunity to take a step back and review questions on particular problem areas, and how the UML may or may not help.

What this book is not

It is important that we make a distinction between developing modelling skills generally, and developing modelling skills specifically with the UML. Something that hampers people in using the UML is not the learning of the notation itself, rather it is confidence in their modelling skills. That is a distinct problem from learning how to model using the UML. Modelling is about recognising the problem and devising an appropriate approach – one of which might be to apply the UML in one or more areas to help to solve, or at least clarify, the problem. This book in itself cannot teach you to model, though by exploring its case studies and attempting the questions and activities we suggest, we believe that your modelling skills will consequently improve.

How should you use this book?

The book is structured in three key parts, with two appendices containing supporting material:

Part One discusses the UML in the context of its use. Whilst it reviews the UML, it concentrates on providing a motivation for its application later in the book. For those with little confidence in UML basics, we also provide summaries of its notation and semantics as appendices.

Part Two contains four case studies, which are diverse and form the heart of the book. The majority of UML textbooks currently available seem to address either the business modelling or software engineering communities. Since the UML notation aims to bridge communities, we consider it important through this book to try and make this point by demonstrating the UML in the role of a general problem solving and communication language. This means keeping the use of the notation simple when possible and applying the UML extensions when necessary.

Part Three tries to pull together the lessons of the earlier sections and to stimulate reflection on how a modelling study can provide concrete benefits. In endeavouring to apply the UML, it is beneficial to do so within the framework of a process or methodology. This topic is first introduced in section one, but we now explore it in a more systematic way. It is difficult to compare and evaluate methodologies. It is therefore difficult for an organisation to determine whether a particular methodology addresses their needs. This section introduces the *CMM for Software* as a framework to evaluate and compare popular process models.

Appendices contain additional reference material concerning the UML notation and semantics and tools to support its use.

We hope you will want to read the book from cover to cover, but we also understand that many readers will be looking for specific help. Where possible we try to indicate how you can quickly find your own route and Chapter 1 contains a route map for this purpose.

There are a number of special features used throughout the book, which try to draw you into reflection on what you are reading, to supplement your learning. Special symbols are placed in the margins to help you spot these sections.

Supplementary material

We had to leave out a lot of the material that we have accumulated over the last five years, to keep this book to a manageable size. We have put most of that material, including our answers to some of the questions we ask, thoughts on tools, links to other useful material and partial case studies using other features, on a Web site. You can access this at our own local Web site (http://www.macs.hw.ac.uk/~umlbook) which also contains a link to the material hosted by the publisher.

Tools often come up in connection with modelling and the application of the UML. They can be at times both an asset and a distraction. In this book we do not advocate the use of a specific tool. In fact we used more than one to prepare our diagrams, including Rational Rose and Microsoft Word's drawing capabilities. Many of them are on our Web site, along with many additional diagrams not included here.

Acknowledgements

The original idea for this book would never have come to fruition without the enthusiastic support of Alfred Waller, our commissioning editor. We would also like to acknowledge the hundreds of students and evening class members who were subjected to early versions of some of this material. They gave us valuable feedback and, crucially, confidence that we were getting some things right in our approach. To all of these, many thanks.

Rob Pooley and Pauline Wilcox, August 2003

Part One

Introductory Material and Background

1

Introduction

Since you have obtained a copy of this book and have started reading it, we assume that you already have an interest in UML. This chapter provides an introduction and a discussion of what we hope you will gain from reading this book and from working through the various activities and questions that we set for you along the way. You will quickly see that this book has a fairly strong participation ethic.

We start this chapter by discussing the motivation for the book and particularly the motivation for making Unified Modelling Language (UML) its focus rather than any other graphical modelling notation.

This chapter also includes a detailed discussion of the structure of the book and the importance of the various case studies that we have included. We think the book has a logical sequential ordering, and can therefore be read from start to finish. However, we realise that there may be particular points that you want to dip in and out of and we would encourage you to make use of this material to your own advantage. We hope that the material discussed in this introductory chapter will help you to find your own route.

1.1 Motivation for this book

This book is not just about UML. Its overall concern is to look at ways of improving communication in system analysis and design, in order to clarify and solve problems through modelling. UML is a notation (or tool, technique, mechanism, if you prefer) that we employ towards the goal of defining and understanding a **problem** so that we can move forwards to identify a **solution**.

You can equip yourself with the latest tools and technology, but none of these help you if you are not supported by good problem solving skills. A primary concern of this book is modelling as a whole. This does not just software system modelling, but business level modelling too. Basically, whatever level of modelling concerns us. Modelling provides a general skill set that can help the understanding, communication and resolution of problems.

There are many important reasons for writing a book that addresses general modelling issues. One of our key motivations is the linking of business and IT systems modelling. Today's technology provides amazing capabilities, and the future potential is tremendous. The application of such technologies allows us to design and implement some highly complex and capable systems. The difficulty that still appears to dog the IT industry is ensuring that we develop and deploy the *right* system. By this we mean the system that will really make the users' life easier, and help the business succeed.

Understanding where systems are being deployed, who uses them, how new systems need to integrate with existing systems and what specific business tasks they support are the keys to implementing a successful information system. This must begin with the realm of business modelling – ensuring that we have an appropriate understanding of the business before we do anything that might affect it. We try to give due emphasis to this in our choice of case studies and in our discussion of them.

At the same time, there are tremendous problems in sharing lower level design issues and solutions. Underpinning many of today's developments in IT are kernel systems to allow user applications to be built on top of sophisticated hardware technologies. Internet applications running over mobile phone networks provide a very good example. The design of these low level systems, such as Wireless Access Protocol or WAP networking, requires sophisticated ways of sharing issues of timing and control in systems built from both software and hardware. UML has had to develop ways of dealing with these and now provides a mechanism for including them explicitly. Again we look at ways of addressing these concerns through appropriate examples.

1.2   Motivation for the choice of UML

There are numerous textbooks that discuss UML notation and its use with regard to particular application domains (software engineering, hardware design and business modelling for example). This book addresses practical issues faced by people in adopting UML. This is reflected in the its title, the aim being to assist the reader in *applying* UML rather than just *learning* UML.

UML is usually accepted to be a significant contribution to the world of computing and IT. The Object Management Group (OMG) claim that "*the Unified Modeling Language (UML) is a language for specifying, visualizing, constructing and documenting the artifacts of software systems, as well as for business modeling and other non-software systems*". The importance of the notation is shared both in academia and industry. A quick scan through job advertisements shows that UML skills are very much sought after, as well being a rich area for consultancy.   A similar scan through calls for participation in academic conferences shows that many have added streams and sessions on how UML fits that conference's special concerns,

Although the OMG description makes UML sound like the solution to all of our problems, it is undoubtedly a notation specifically aiming to enhance and improve communication between people. As a human activity, communication is something that we need to continually strive to improve – it is a key area in which we fail daily. Whilst we are unlikely to ever fully resolve this problem, we can adopt and refine techniques that may help us along the way.

Let us begin with the somewhat simple, but never-the-less true statement of what UML is in the following *key point*.

KEY POINT	UML definition	UML is a notation that supports the communication and documentation of models	

People therefore read books and attend courses and gain an appreciation of UML notation. They learn about the merits of use case modelling and its associated notation; they learn about class modelling and associated UML notation; they may go on to learn about the modelling of interactions and states. This is fine, but our experience shows that this is only ever part of the learning process. You can learn a new skill/technique, but applying it for real raises all sorts of problems. These problems are the motivation for this book – they can be summarised under the question headings shown in the following *key point* table below.

KEY POINT	How do I use UML?	This is a question often asked by people once they have started to get their head around the notation and wonder where the magic spell is.
	What should I do?	People often want to know which diagram to use for which problem. This is almost always the wrong question to ask.
	How can I get a neat solution?	People are often seeking an impractical neat outcome from their UML modelling. This is an inappropriate goal of a modelling activity.

These questions are based on misconceptions concerning UML notation, because often, from the marketing literature, people's expectations of UML itself are too high. They also arise because of misunderstandings regarding modelling. Our answers are explored below:

How do I use UML?

Having taken the time and trouble to become familiar with UML notation, people are often left asking the question "how do I use it?" They have learned about UML use case modelling notation, UML class modelling notation, UML interaction modelling notation etc. Unfortunately each is often learned and viewed in isolation or in the form of examples which are already complete. In fact, in applying UML the real power comes from cross-referencing the various models represented in these diagrams. In order to be able to do that, the UML modeller has to be able to see and understand the possible links between the various diagrams and their elements.

The solution to this particular problem may be found by choosing an appropriate *process*, often described as a *methodology*, which provides a framework for tackling a problem. That framework may suggest a particular process model, using a number of stages or phases, and may advocate the use of particular techniques or notations, such as UML. This is particularly useful in dealing with the sub-question, "Where do I start?"

However, just as UML in itself is not the answer to all of our prayers, neither is a methodology if applied without thought. In particular, if the goal becomes finding a methodology that allows us to use UML then this can lead to an inappropriate choice. Choosing an approach because it advocates the use of a notation is not a good reason in itself. Poor choice of a methodology leads to that methodology being blamed when things don't quite turn out as people had hoped. Early enthusiasm for object oriented approaches was followed by several claims of its deficiencies, from those who had applied it blindly. Valid reasons for choosing an approach will be looked at initially in Chapter 4, with a more thorough treatment being given in the third section of this book.

This book tries to show examples of UML being applied in a range of case studies. These may present ways of using UML that you had not previously considered.

What should I do?
What should I do?

People feel the need to pigeon-hole UML diagrams. They therefore want to know, "If I'm doing analysis/design activity X, concerning problem Y, what UML notation (diagrams) should I produce?" People often focus on what they *should* be doing, according to some inflexible rule, rather than asking themselves, "What is helpful at this point?" So, for example, if you are working to analyse an existing system (business process, piece of software or hardware) in order to find out how it works, then what you are *wanting to represent* will determine the appropriate UML notation to use. For example, if you are trying to capture the high level requirements that the system is satisfying then a use case diagram may help. If you are wanting to model the static structure of the system then a class diagram may help.

This is something that we will endeavour to highlight throughout the case studies in this book, i.e. focussing on the problem that we want to address and using this to showcase a particular subset of UML rather than focussing on examples of the diagrams for their own sake.

How can I get a neat solution?
How can I get a neat solution?

There is a further problem that often gets in the way of applying UML successfully. People are often looking for, what they consider to be, a tidy solution. They therefore would like a single use case diagram, a single class diagram etc. that *reflects everything they need to know* – because this is a neat and satisfactory outcome. Regrettably, this is not often a practical starting aim. The reality is that a series of diagrams focussing on different elements, views or levels of the system is probably more useful. These may have to be continually revised as ideas are developed. Through this book we will be exploring why that is the case.

Having elaborated on the above questions, we present no more specific answers at this point. It is hoped that such answers, along with many others, will emerge from the remainder of this book.

At this point we would like to encourage you to try the following activity before you carry on with the rest of this chapter. You can do this just as a mental exercise, but as with most activities, there is additional benefit to be had from taking a blank piece of paper and trying to get some of your ideas and thoughts down on it. We can convince ourselves that we have all manner of things straight and understood in our heads – but we find that the act of writing things down really focusses the mind. Compare your answers with your experience of UML as you read further.

Q: *Take a few minutes to think about a particular project you have been involved in, or have read about, that used some sort of graphical notation (possibly in-house informal doodles). What was the nature of the problem being analysed? Can you characterise the nature of the problem being addressed? How did the particular notation help you (or you in relation to other members of the project team)? What problems were experienced with the notation?*

1.3   Structure of this book

This book has three main parts. **Part One** is made up of **Chapters 1** to **4**, **Part Two** is **Chapters 5** to **9**, **Part Three** is **chapters 10** and **11**. There are also two appendices, which are there for you to refer to, as you need.

These sections all concern the application of UML. We focus on the discussion of practical issues faced in using that notation. It is not, therefore, a book that introduces UML notation *per se*. However, we consider that it is infeasible to launch into a detailed discussion of case studies without some review of the notation and an understanding of the current position with regard to changes to UML. You may also find that we use it in slightly different ways to those with which you are familiar.

Part One is there to allow you to become attuned to our approach. **Chapter 1** tries to motivate and describe the book. **Chapter 2** provides a simple introductory case study that models a bank. This provides an opportunity to examine what we consider to be the core UML notation (if you consider that you are already familiar with UML notation then feel free to skip this chapter). **Chapter 3** reviews the development of UML notation itself. It explains the way in which UML is expected to develop in the future, in particular the recent emphasis on the so called *profile* mechanism. We think that it is important to reflect on some of the recent history of developments in object-oriented notations that have contributed to UML. This allows us to see UML in the context of where it has come from and where it is going – it is not yet a silver bullet that will solve all of our problems. Let's be honest, we don't think it ever will be, but through this book we hope to give you a more rounded understanding of the notation and the ways in which it can be applied to good effect.

When first exploring UML, people are often uncomfortable with learning that UML itself is just a notation, merely a language that acts as a tool or a technique. Beyond the rules of syntax and semantics, defined in UML standard, there are no prescribed rules for how it should be used. We pick up on this subject in **Chapter 4** by returning to the importance and relevance of systematic approaches or methodologies to the successful application of UML. Methodologies are something that people often adopt without thinking *what* they are *using* and *why*, yet this can have a major influence on the success of application of UML. Specific examples of current and influential approaches, some more rigid than others, are something we will return to later in the book, specifically in **Part Three** where we will introduce an example framework for comparing the respective methodologies to highlight their respective strengths and weaknesses.

Part Two contains the core material of this book. Our approach is to explore the application of UML within a range of different problem areas. We do this through a series of diverse case studies – each case study has been carefully chosen to illustrate the application of UML to the particular type of problem, and examine the benefits and pitfalls thereof. We explore the significance of each in **Section 1.4**, below.

Part Three concerns the importance of an organisation making appropriate choices about which methodology to apply. Mostly this is about recognising the importance of process. **Chapter 10** introduces the Capability Maturity Model (CMM) for Software. The CMM is a framework which represents a path of improvements that are recommended for organisations that want to increase their process capability. Whilst this is interesting in itself, in **Chapter 11** we go on to consider how the CMM can be applied as a framework to compare the suitability of a range of methodologies. This provides an opportunity to learn about characteristics that you might look for when aiming to adopt or adapt an established methodology.

1.4   Case studies

Case studies are a key part of this book. Previously discussed, we've devoted all four chapters of **Part Two** to them. It is important that we take some time here to explain the purpose of these case studies in general, as well as to explain the range and diversity of the actual case studies that we have included in the book.

There are a number of different reasons for choosing a case study. Consider, for example, the following two alternative views:

1.   The case study may itself be the important thing. This means that giving sufficient detail of the problem and its area is an overriding factor. For example, if you want

to learn about e-commerce then it would be helpful to explore a case study that used such a system or business as its core material.

2.   The case study may be simply a vehicle to explore particular points about modelling. Now the facts of the case study itself are not so crucial – they only need to be detailed and accurate enough for the intended purpose. For example, if you wanted to see an example of a use case diagram, then the fact that the subject of the use case diagram is Web-based retailing may be less important.

We would argue that the case studies we have chosen for this book primarily fall into the second category. The reason for using a variety of case studies is to present you with a variety of different perspectives and scenarios requiring different subsets of UML notation and a different approaches to its application. They provide contrasting and complementary examples of the notation in practice and show UML being used in ways that you may not have previously considered, along with a discussion of the benefits we felt were realised. Of course we could have added any number of additional case studies. What we have attempted to do is to pick a number that each have a significantly different story to tell.

In order to make the most of these case studies, and the book in general, it is important that you try to engage with the material as much as possible. Modelling generally, and the application of UML specifically, are practical activities – it is important to learn by doing. In the context of this book that means taking the time to consider the questions and activities that we present in each chapter.

We have emphasised that this book does not primarily aim to try and teach you how to model, as if there could be some formula or trick, guaranteed to work. Instead, the aim, through the case studies, is to present examples UML being applied, with discussion of how and why it is being used. In this way we hope to help you to improve your modelling skills with UML and in general. No book in itself can teach you to model, but by exploring case studies and attempting the questions and activities we suggest, we believe your modelling skills will inevitably improve.

Whenever we are learning to apply a new skill, we are inevitably distracted by concerns that we are not doing it *right*. In the context of this book, and the activities in which we hope you will become engaged, this concern may lead further to a worry that the model you are developing is *wrong*. There are certainly ongoing activities in the field of Computer Science where people strive to develop model checkers, so that at some time in the future we may prove the *correctness* of a model being developed. Those engaged in this effort are themselves concerned that UML lacks sufficiently strict rules to support such formal verification. Let us be clear that this is not a concern of this book.

We consider it more appropriate to consider how *helpful* the model is, not whether it conforms to some abstract set of rules. Modelling is a creative activity, involving intuition, experience and communication of ideas and concerns. Actually, we have found mistakes in some of our favourite examples while developing this book. Those flawed examples don't seem to have prevented us teaching the key ideas of this subject to literally hundreds of students over several years. (We have, however, tried to fix them for you! Let us know if you spot any we have missed.)

There are two elements to try and separate out:

- Appropriate and correct use of UML notation

- Appropriate and helpful model

Let us examine these two perspectives further. The first one requires an understanding of UML notation – the syntax and semantics. This book primarily assumes that you are coming to this material with at least a basic understanding of the core UML notation. (We refer you to read **Chapter 2** as a refresher and to the appendices for more detail.) Consider though, that it is rarely important to apply all of the notation to a given model – the aim with most modelling activities is to keep things as simple as possible – so you should not be trying to shoe-horn in all of the UML notation you can think of. Detail in the notation is there for when you need it – the key skill is to work out what it is that you need and what will help most in a given situation.

KEY POINT	Should you add more detail? If in doubt, create a simple model that you understand and that you can explain to others, rather than elaborating with information that is open to doubt. Notes are a mechanism for recording possibilities for future debate.

The second point concerns the usefulness of the model itself as we develop it. We've lost count of the number of people who come up to us, present us with a few pages of UML notation and ask us, "*Is this model right?*" They are immediately dismayed when we reply by saying (as is our usual response), "*Well it depends – what exactly are you trying to show?*"

This is a stumbling block because they have not thought about what they are really trying to do in developing the model. This is because developing a model is always a learning experience – the things you discover through the experience are not always the things you set out to examine. This is just a natural aspect of modelling. When people consider their own model, explaining to themselves and others what it is that they are trying to represent, they are forced to question the model. Does it reflect what they had hoped for?

KEY POINT	Is the model right? Our general advice is that if the model raises questions and provokes discussion then it is serving a helpful purpose.

These are points that we will return to in examining case studies in subsequent chapters – our advice for now is to try and engage with the material and attempt the exercises and questions that we pose as you work through the material and enjoy the learning experience.

At this point let us describe the four case studies that we have chosen to use in this text, and our reasons for doing so. You may want to jump ahead to one which matches your current concerns, and we certainly don't want to try to stop you. Just remember that they are there to help us understand the modelling, not the application area.

Here are outline of the general subject covered by each case study, highlighting the key characteristics in each case, focussing on the modelling issues.

Chapter 5: The Trusty Car Company
This chapter considers a case study that involves elements of business and systems modelling. The following are key characteristics of this case study:
- Identifying appropriate problem scope
- Clarification of business requirements
- Iterative nature of modelling
- Cross-references between UML diagrams across the system development lifecycle.
- Alternative views of a problem using the same UML notation.

Chapter 6: Playing Games
This chapter considers a case study at a higher level of abstraction. Its focus is to introduce the design of a multi-player game framework. This case study has the following key characteristics:
- Reuse (including the notation of patterns)
- Abstraction and postponing implementation decisions.

Chapter 7: Road Junction
This chapter considers a problem area where timing and synchronisation are important. The key characteristics of this case study can be outlined as follows:
- Timing and synchronisation information
- Importance of modelling interactions and their implications
- Moving towards implementation.

Chapter 8: Supporting Distributed Working
This chapter considers a case study leading back to the consideration of processes – and acknowledging that working practices exist which influence the ways in which people may work with technology. The case study concerns modelling the way that modellers work (we trust you will see the relevance of this subject). In particular, how modellers may be affected when working in a distributed environment (e.g. where modellers are in different locations) and ways in which they might apply UML. Key characteristics are:
- People working in distributed environment
- Disposable modelling
- Recognising and modelling scenarios of usage.

Table 1.1 identifies the four case studies and the elements of notation that are covered in each. You may find this helpful if you are particularly concerned with an issue of notation, but you might also want to consult **Appendix A**. There is significant crossover with the same type of diagram being used in each of the different case studies. This is important as it shows the diagram type being used in different contexts, highlighting a different application of UML.

	Trusty Car Company	Playing Games	Road Junction	Supporting Distributed Working
Use Case diagram	✓	✓	✓	✓
Class diagram	✓	✓	✓	✓
Sequence diagram	✓	✓	✓	✓
Collaboration diagram		✓	✓	✓
Deployment diagram		✓		✓
Statechart		✓	✓	
Package diagram				
Activity diagram	✓			✓
Profile for schedulability, performance and time			✓	
Business Modelling	✓			

Table 1.1: UML usage across case studies

2

A Complete Example

This chapter provides an introduction to UML in the form of a complete case study. The case study concerns a simple model of a bank and its offering of two different types of account. In the previous chapter we discussed the use of case studies, and the way that we explore UML with a number of them in this book. Now we want to provide a simple framework within which to introduce some key points of UML notation. More importantly, perhaps, it allows us to start to look at *how* UML notation can be applied to help us define and understand a particular problem.

Why then did we choose this case study? As mentioned earlier, this books aims to reach a wider audience by considering applications of UML to both business modelling and software engineering. The bank case study is chosen to help us see how UML can express ideas in both areas. At the same time we wanted a subject that you could relate to easily and is not baffling when the terms and scenarios are presented. For this reason we introduced a case study of a simple bank and the two types of accounts that it offers. In our classroom teaching, experience has shown that this is successful, in that people come to the subject having an understanding of the case study subject. Thus they are in a position to make certain assumptions and ask questions, both of which are necessary skills to develop in any modelling activity.

2.1 Case study introduction

In the previous chapter we talked about the importance of becoming actively engaged in the material. We want to re-emphasise here the benefits of trying things out for yourself, so that you *learn by doing*. So here is your first real opportunity – try out the following activity! Do keep it brief – we don't intend that you should spend an excessive amount of time on any of the activities that we suggest. In the case of the following activity, its purpose is to let you form a few ideas of your own about the case study before moving on to look at the various models that we develop with UML.

A: Take a couple of minutes to read through the description of the introductory bank account case study shown in figure 2.1. Try to pull out the key things that we might want to represent in a model of the bank as described. To give you a little more focus, we suggest that you concentrate on identifying requirements. If you have programmed in Java or C++ you might also find it natural to start to look for candidate classes and operations/methods. You will be able to compare your own ideas with those we present throughout this chapter.

You are asked to design a system to handle current and savings accounts for a bank. Accounts are assigned to one or more customers, who may make deposits or withdraw money. Each type of account earns interest on the current balance held in it. Current accounts may have negative balances (overdrafts) and then interest is deducted. Rates of interest are different for each type of account. On a savings account, there is a maximum amount that can be withdrawn in one transaction.

Bank employees may check any account that is held at their branch. They are responsible for invoking the addition of interest and for issuing statements at the correct times.

A money transfer is a short-lived record of an amount that has been debited from one account and has to be credited to another. A customer may create such a transfer from their account to any other. Transfers within a branch happen immediately, while those between branches take three days.

Figure 2.1: Introductory description of the bank

2.2 Application of UML

Remember as we work through this case study that it is a vehicle to examine key elements of UML notation. Using it as a basis, we will illustrate the models shown in the following *UML used in this chapter* information box, thereby demonstrating each particular component of UML notation.

UML Used in this Chapter		
	USE CASE DIAGRAM	to examine and capture requirements of the business and therefore of some system that may potentially support the business.
	CLASS DIAGRAM	to start to examine system structure.
	INTERACTION DIAGRAM	to express system dynamics.
	ACTIVITY DIAGRAM	to illustrate dependencies in system and also business process modelling.

The UML diagrams described in the above information box represent, in our opinion, the core of notation that the typical modeller will need. This specifically excludes the following; packages, deployment diagrams, state charts and various extensions. We are not saying that these additional parts of UML are not useful, merely that they do not readily fit within the scope of this introductory case study. Most of these additional elements of UML will be discussed in subsequent case studies to show their relevance.

The point, in what follows, is not to give a blow by blow account of the notation. We aim to use it to provide a useful example of the use of each diagram in a particular context to see how the diagrams combine together to help develop a richer model. For a more detailed account of UML syntax and semantics we recommend that you consult Appendix A of this text.

A: If you are already familiar with some or all of the UML diagrams mentioned in the *UML used in this chapter* information box you might want to experiment by drawing your own examples with regard to the case study described in figure 2.1. Remember that the aim is not that you end up with a set of diagrams that look like the ones that we introduce – the point is that you use the diagrams (ours or your own) to shape your thinking and determine a series of questions.

2.2.1 Use Case Diagrams

Nearly all object oriented design methods now incorporate use case models to represent requirements. One of the three original contributors to UML (Chapter 3 will provide a brief history of UML), Ivar Jacobsen, was the main author of the use case approach to requirements capture. We consider here the key characteristics of a use case diagram, and specifically how this helps us develop a use case model of the bank given the limited description we currently have in figure 2.1.

A use case model represents the *external view* of the system being modelled. A use case model can be shown as a use case diagram, but remember that the diagram is not the model.

Q: *Before continuing with this section, spend a moment to reflect on the point we are making here. Why is the model not the same thing as the diagram? This question will be addressed in the text as you read on.*

Here we start examination of the bank by developing a use case model. There are many alternative opinions on whether to take a use case driven approach, or whether in fact we should start with a class diagram. We do not take a high minded view in this book that one approach should be taken to the exclusion of the other. It is a matter of considering what you know, what you want to achieve and the other team members who may be involved. Our own experience is that, as object-oriented thinkers we tend to develop our ideas in tandem. There are many good reasons for considering the use case model early. Specifically, it helps to identify the model scope or boundary; what is inside and outside our area of interest? As simple as this question sounds, it is something that is often not considered early in a modelling activity. A reminder of the three main notation elements in the use case diagram can be found in the following *use case notation reminde*r box.

	ACTORS	The roles adopted by those participating.
Use Case Notation Reminder	**USE CASES**	High level activities/requirements to be supported by the business/system.
	LINKS	Which actors are involved in which use cases.

16 A Complete Example

Using the notation elements described in the above information box, consider the diagram in figure 2.2, which presents a *possible* use case diagram of the bank capturing the main requirements.

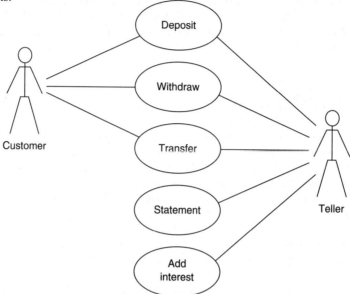

Figure 2.2: Initial use case diagram for bank

The first thing you can see is the simplicity of the notation. There are five use cases represented in the diagram, each shown by the oval with the use case name written inside the oval. There are two actors shown, **Customer** and **Teller**. These actors are shown to be associated with a number of use cases, because they are connected by lines.

KEY POINT	Given the name of the diagram it is not surprising that people are often more focussed on the use cases. However, identification of actors is a key benefit of the use case diagram. Even a diagram with a single use case has a purpose if it helps the modeller focus on the interfaces to the system, since these are what the actor notation and the linking lines represent – namely, some thing (person, IT system, item of hardware etc.) has an interface to the thing (system) we are interested in modelling. This forces us to think clearly about the scope of the system.

At this point it is helpful to have a reminder about key aspects of the actor in a use case diagram. We've listed these in the *all about actors* information box on the following page. Clear identification of actors is a key benefit to come out of a use case modelling exercise. Identification of actors can often be a good way to start the modelling process, since they help to define a boundary to the system/business of interest.

The use case symbol itself indicates a requirement that will supply benefit or value to an actor. Within each use case there must be a description of what this requirement does for the actor – this comes back to our previous point that the diagram itself is not *the model*.

The model may require more information/detail than can be contained in a single diagram. A use case model could therefore comprise a number of use case diagrams and a number of other diagrams and text-based pieces of documentation, which explain and elaborate on the use case diagram.

All About Actors	An actor indicates an external person or system that is involved in a use case.
	The same person or system may play the role of more than one actor, depending on the context.
	An actor may be a set of roles, which are related.
	An actor may be involved in more than one use case.
	One actor is normally the initiator of each use case.

Is the use case diagram sufficient on its own without further elaboration or documentation? As much as we advocate the use of diagrams and their expressive power, the use cases eventually need some further elaboration. We've reached an appropriate point to consider *how* some of this additional descriptive and explanatory information concerning the use case model can be recorded. There are a number of techniques available to us, and which one is appropriate will depend on the degree of documentation/explanation required as well as agreement within a project team regarding the appropriate level of working.

A number of common approaches to describing use cases and use case diagrams are summarised in the following *mechanisms to describe use cases* information box.

Mechanisms to describe use cases	By English descriptions. For clarity use active voice, present tense, e.g. Active - Hazel eats an apple a day ☺ Passive - each day an apple is eaten by Hazel ☹
	UML State charts
	UML Activity diagrams
	UML Interaction diagrams
	Any other means you prefer!

While a key purpose of this book is to advocate the use of diagrams wherever possible to *reduce* the amount of text that people have to read through, there are times when text plays an important and necessary role. We do not rule it out completely, and a text-based description features as the first option in the above information box as a means to describe a use case. The aim in the text-based description is brevity and clarity. To develop the model of the bank further, let us now consider an example of a use case description. The particular example defines the behaviour within the use case called **Deposit**. Take a moment to read through the use case description in figure 2.3.

The customer passes over to the bank an amount of money, in some combination of cash and cheques. The customer specifies which account is to be updated. The teller checks the money and authorises the updating of the relevant account.

If the money is incorrect or the account does not exist the teller informs the customer, returns the money and the account is not updated.

Figure 2.3: Deposit use case description for bank

Within the use case description we can clearly identify a number of facts. For example, that the **Customer** is the actor who *initiates* the use case and that there are certain *inputs* and *outcomes*. We can also identify a range of *exceptions*, where the outcome is not the normal or usual outcome that we would expect. These are all key bits of information to look for in describing a use case. The description in figure 2.3 clearly communicates key points concerning the use case, without an excessive amount of text.

The key things to look for when describing use cases are summarised in the following *describing use cases* information box, along with examples from the **Deposit** use case description (from figure 2.3).

Describing Use Cases	**INITIATOR**	The customer is the actor that initiates the deposit.
	INPUTS	The inputs to the use case are identified, i.e. account number, money and customer identification.
	OUTCOMES	The outcomes are identified, i.e. account updated.
	EXCEPTIONS	Two exceptions are identified and the alternative outcomes are given, i.e. money incorrect or invalid account number results in teller reporting back to customer and no account updated.

It is important that the use case description is *adequate* for the users to agree that it is accurate, without becoming a design.

Q: *Why is it important to avoid going down to the design level at this point? This* *question will be addressed in the text as you read on.*

You might well be asking yourself at this point why we did not include the extra descriptive detail of figure 2.3 at the start of this chapter in the initial case study outlined in figure 2.1? Perhaps you consider it a bit of a cheat, that we have not presented all of the case study information in the description at the beginning of the chapter? Well, consider for yourself how realistic it is to have *all* the necessary information you need at the start of any modelling activity. The reality is that you find extra information out as you go along. At the outset it is likely that you won't know everything you will need to – you make assumptions, you raise questions that need to be clarified. This is all part of the natural modelling process. So we don't consider introducing extra information at this point a cheat ... now on with the problem in hand.

At this point we have an initial use case diagram and a description of one of the use cases. We are now going to look at how we can develop a system structure to support these requirements – we will do this using the class diagram notation.

A: Before going on with the next section, you might like to spend a little time and try to provide a text-based description of the remaining use cases in the developing model. Remember that there is probably information missing, so you need to be able to make reasoned assumptions, or raise questions that you would want to ask. This is still a useful exercise even given the incomplete level of information. Solutions to this activity can be found on the Web site which accompanies this book (details of which were given in the preface).

Before moving onto the next section, the earlier question suggested you consider why, in use case modelling, it is recommended that you avoid going down to the design level. There are a number of points to consider. The main case against developing design ideas is that it introduces a bias into the modelling activity – which may be unwarranted. Many of us will have worked on projects and in environments where certain project members (on the client side or within the project team) will have a preconceived vision of the solution, the chosen technology etc. Apart from anything else, there is a certain human characteristic that will see many of us try and skip ahead a few steps and leap to a solution.

The natural human tendency is to try and cut short the business and systems analysis phases and resulting requirements elicitation – because, as IT professionals, we *know* what the customer needs and we can jump right to it. Does that sound familiar? It is fundamentally not advisable, and it demonstrates a lack of process and rigor. On the other hand, there are times when certain design and implementation criteria that may well be known at the outset of the project. If such constraints exist, then it is sensible to incorporate them clearly in early modelling work. As ever, then, there is no hard and fast rule, though we hope that you will consider this point in your use case modelling activities.

2.2.2 Class Diagram

At this point let us assume that the requirements have been satisfactorily explored, so now we want to examine a static structure that could support these requirements. We start to build a class model. As with most modelling activities there is an incremental approach that we ideally take – it is unlikely that we will simply arrive at a satisfactory model with our first attempt.

A common initial problem that people encounter with class modelling is knowing exactly where and how to begin. Unfortunately, there is no magic solution to this problem, that will work in all situations. As you gain experience with class modelling and modelling in the given business domain, your modelling efforts will be influenced by previous projects. You will, for example, more readily see an initial set of candidate classes and associations between them. This is basically a form of pattern recognition based on your own learning. The study of more formal design patterns can also help, in which case you are applying the experience of others.

At this point though, assuming minimal experience with class modelling and knowledge of the domain, we suggest a simple text-based analysis technique. This text, or *noun clause,* analysis can help the modeller to make a start with the class modelling activity. By following a fairly simple set of steps we can begin to determine a number of candidate classes and objects. This set of steps is shown in the *steps for finding candidate classes and objects* information box which follows.

Steps for finding candidate classes and objects	Step 1: We can identify objects in our problem statement by looking for nouns and noun phrases.
	Step 2: Each of these can be underlined and becomes a candidate for an object in our solution.
	Step 3: We can eliminate some objects by some simple rules.

In applying these rules it is important to make sure that our objects fit in with our use cases, thus staying within the system requirements and scope. Apart from being good practice, this highlights a link point between different models and UML diagrams. This is something that often presents a difficulty to people learning to use UML, as connections between the different diagrams do not always seem obvious to them.

LINK POINT	There should be some connection between use cases and classes. The classes need to provide the necessary structure to support the requirements outlined in the use cases. It may be feasible to map a series of classes to a use case and vice versa.

A: Take a couple of minutes to re-examine the Bank Account case study introduced earlier in this chapter. Have a go at identifying what you think may be candidate classes and objects based on the approach identified in the three steps shown in the *steps for finding candidate classes and objects* information box, i.e. identification of nouns and noun phrases. A solution to this activity will be presented as this case study develops (so try and do the activity without looking too far ahead).

When you have had a go at the above activity consider our own suggestions for candidate classes. In following steps 1 and 2 of our *steps for finding candidate classes and objects*, we arrived at the initial set of candidates shown in figure 2.4. This is basically a copy of the text from figure 2.1 with possible classes and objects underlined (specifically showing step 2 of the approach outlined earlier). Do not worry at this point if your own approach resulted in more or less items underlined. The point of this approach is that it helps you to make a start and get you over the problem of starting with a blank piece of paper.

You are asked to design a system to handle <u>current and savings accounts</u> for a <u>bank</u>. <u>Accounts</u> are assigned to one or more <u>customers</u>, who may make <u>deposits</u> or withdraw <u>money</u>. Each type of account earns <u>interest</u> on the <u>current balance</u> held in it. Current accounts may have negative balances (<u>overdrafts</u>) and then interest is deducted. <u>Rates of interest</u> are different for each type of account. On a savings account, there is a <u>maximum amount</u> that can be withdrawn in one <u>transaction</u>.

<u>Bank employees</u> may check any account that is held at their <u>branch</u>. They are responsible for invoking the addition of interest and for issuing <u>statements</u> at the <u>correct times</u>.

A <u>money transfer</u> is a short lived <u>record</u> of an <u>amount</u> which has been debited from one account and has to be credited to another. A customer may create such a transfer from their account to any other. Transfers within a branch happen immediately, while those between branches take three <u>days</u>.

Figure 2.4: Identification of candidate classes and objects

Once you have a candidate list of classes and objects you can complete the third of the *steps for finding candidate classes and objects*. This involves carrying out a review of our candidates and eliminating one or more at this stage. There are seven simple rules that we would suggest to help you do this. These are shown in the following information box called *Rules/criteria to refine candidate classes*. The same information box also has a column showing potential classes/objects (from those that we identified in figure 2.4) which might, we would argue, fit these rules.

You may agree or disagree with our choices at this point, but again the main aim is to provide an initial set of candidates that we can work further with. The most important thing is that we can *reason* about the inclusion or exclusion of candidates, so that there is some structure and rigour to our thinking. For example, if we consider a candidate is redundant, then we mean it is catered for elsewhere in another candidate. For example, we suggest that overdraft is an attribute of another class and that account is already dealt with by assuming we will use current account and savings accounts. You may already have some views on the latter point – and be assured we will return to consider this again in a further iteration of the class model.

The point is again not to be overly concerned with trying to get everything right at the outset. We need to make reasoned judgements based on what we currently know and understand. Modellers should always reserve the right to return in order to add or remove model elements at a later stage of the modelling process, as their knowledge and understanding improves.

Rules / Criteria to refine Candidate Classes	**REDUNDANT**	overdraft, account
	VAGUE	amount, money
	EVENT/OPERATION	transaction, deposit
	OUTSIDE SCOPE	bank, days
	META-LANGUAGE	transaction, correct times, record
	ATTRIBUTE	interest, rate of interest, maximum amount, current balance, overdraft
	ACTOR	Check if candidate class is required, or if in fact it is an actor e.g. is **Customer** required as a class?

Consider the point regarding actors. There is an important distinction to be made between an actor, as we identify it on a use case diagram, and an avatar class. In the developing case study we have a **Customer** actor and a **Customer** class. These are not the same thing.

One is a representation of customers inside the system (this is the **Customer** class). You might like to think about this as a computer-based record of a customer. The other is the role of the customer who is, in some way, interacting with the system from the outside. Perhaps you might choose to make this clearer by using separate names. This is, in fact, enforced by certain modelling tools, for example Rational Rose. Our own preference is to use the same name where possible, to reinforce the association between external and internal model components.

KEY POINT	Be clear and consistent in identifying classes and actors where there may be confusion over similarities – in particular clarify where you have actors and associated avatar classes. At this stage in the class modelling exercise it might be appropriate to return to consider the actors identified in the use case model.

Once we have identified an initial set of classes (however that is achieved), we can start to form a graphical representation of them and add associations between them. We do this using UML class diagram notation. As with many other UML diagrams, the class diagram notation supports a wide range of options. Remember that, in a given situation, it is likely that only a subset of that notation will actually be required. We will illustrate this point by developing the class diagram incrementally. At each incremental step we will add further detail to the developing model.

Given the candidate classes that remain (after those we have eliminated in the *Rules/criteria to refine candidate classes* information box), we propose the initial class diagram shown in figure 2.5. This is the simplest form of class diagram that still communicates a useful level of information, namely identifying the classes by name and showing associations between them. Note that we have made some further assumptions by showing the direction of association, with an open arrow head.

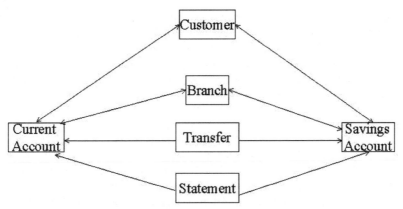

Figure 2.5: Initial class diagram outline

Q: *Consider the initial diagram in figure 2.5. What do you infer about the class Transfer and its association with Current Account and Savings Account classes? This question will be addressed in the text as you read on.*

Taking the diagram in figure 2.5 as a basic framework, the next useful level of detail we would naturally look to add would be to provide a descriptive name for each of the associations. This stage leads to the diagram presented in figure 2.6.

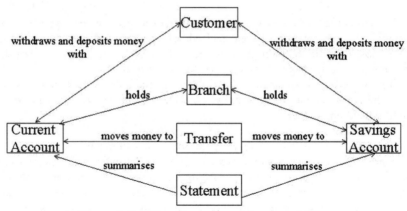

Figure 2.6: Class diagram naming associations

Note that the descriptions of associations are kept as short and simple as possible while still conveying the nature of the relationship between the classes. These can also be revised and revisited as the model develops. Having identified and named associations, the next level of detail to add concerns multiplicity information. To be technical for a moment, this indicates *the degree* of the association and is a very powerful annotation that provides additional information about the underlying data model.

Consider the example in figure 2.7. With the addition of the multiplicity information this diagram now makes specific statements about the underlying data model and the business that it supports. For example, a **Customer** may deposit money with zero or more **Current Accounts**. A **Current Account** may have money deposited by one and only one **Customer**. We could discuss (amongst ourselves or with some actual customers) whether this is the most helpful association to record between an account and a customer.

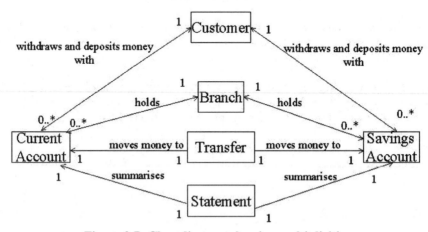

Figure 2.7: Class diagram showing multiplicities

Q: *Consider the class diagram shown in figure 2.7 and the above comments concerning the Customer class and its associations with the Current Account and Savings Account classes. What implications does this have for joint accounts, if any? This question will be addressed in the text as you read on.*

Having added all of the above information to the class diagram, we could start to elaborate on the detail *inside* each of the classes. For example, consider the additional detail added to the **Current Account** class in figure 2.8. This further refined diagram shows how the classifier notation can be further expanded and annotated to show attributes and operations inside the class. Here we tentatively suggest a single private attribute, and three public operations that allow the balance to be manipulated.

If you reach the point of being satisfied with the classes at a high level, then looking inside to try and identify at least key attributes and operations can help you to test out the developing model. If you cannot identify initial attributes and operations, perhaps there are questions to be asked about the validity of the class within the model? This may lead you to refine the model further, or at least raise a series of questions that need to be asked.

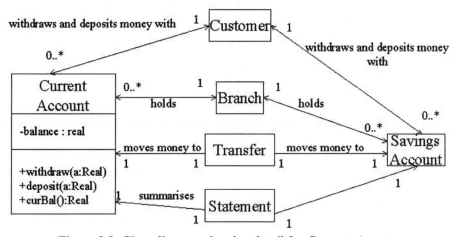

Figure 2.8: Class diagram showing detail for Current Account

A: As a helpful activity at this point, consider expanding one or more of the classes shown in figure 2.8 (or in your own model if you are developing your own variation). By this we mean, carry out a similar exercise to that shown on the **Current Account** class – itentify one or more attributes and operations, choosing appropriate names and assigning access levels. Solutions to this activity can be found on the Web site which accompanies this book.

Each of the class diagrams that we have introduced in figures 2.5 through 2.8 represents a useful level of detail; each one in itself may be appropriate depending on the purpose for which it is drawn. Just because you are applying additional UML notation and adding further and further detail does not make a diagram more useful – it might in fact make it too complicated and distract from a number of fundamental points that need to be resolved.

Consider how in the class model so far we have two classes that represent accounts – **Current Account** and **Savings Account**. Do we really need both of these, or can we represent an alternative design by introducing generalisation into the model? Consider the example shown in figure 2.9, which contains a class diagram illustrating just the classes we are concerned with (again, why show more detail in a diagram than we are really interested in?).

The picture presented shows all common attributes and operations having been extracted from **Current Account** and **Savings Account** and placed in a generalisation class called **Account**. Note further that we are making an implementation decision in the diagram by indicating that any **Account** object created must be of one of the two specializations because the class itself is shown to be an abstract class (shown by the use of the tag {abstract} below the class name) and as such objects of that class type cannot be instantiated. The withdraw operation is also shown in italics inside the **Account** class, indicating that it is an abstract operation which must be implemented in any specialisation class.

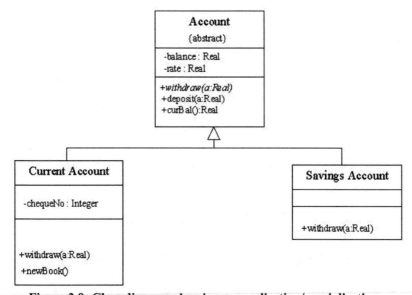

Figure 2.9: Class diagram showing generalisation/specialisation

We can, of course, take this additional information about the generalisation and specialisation associations and update our original class diagram. The resulting class diagram is shown in figure 2.10, showing the new **Account** class and its generalisation relationship with its two specialisations. All associations with other classes are found to be with the generalised class **Account**, which is often a clue that we are right to use a generalisation. Note that again, in terms of representing relevant information we do not consider it essential in this diagram to show the internal details of classes.

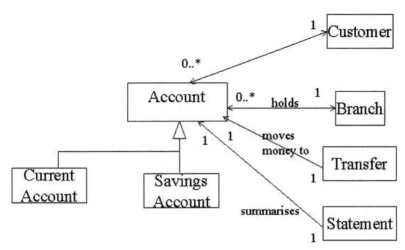

Figure 2.10: Revised class diagram with Account class

It is important as the class model develops that it is repeatedly checked back against the requirements and that we ensure that appropriate business processes and rules are supported. The multiplicity information is a very powerful indicator of business rules.

Consider the earlier question posed in this section concering the association between **Customer** and **Current Account** (or **Savings Account**). The multiplicity information would seem to indicate that either type of account can be associated with one and only one **Customer**. This would seem to explicity rule out the support for joint accounts. This is a fairly fundamental business issue that needs to be resolved, as it could have far reaching implications for any system to support the business. It is important that at each stage of the modelling process we keep checking what questions the model makes us ask about the supported business processes and rules. We will talk further about business modelling later in this chapter.

Another question earlier in this section asked you to consider what you understood about the **Transfer** class and its associations with **Current Account** and **Savings Account**. Our experience from using this example in classroom-based teaching is that the layout introduced in figure 2.5 leads people to draw various conclusions about the role of the **Transfer** class simply because it is positioned *between* the classes representing the two types of account. The implication is that a transfer takes place between a **Current Account** and a **Savings Account**. Whilst this may be true (according to the business rules of the bank), the transfer could also occur between two instances of the **Current Account** or two instances of the **Savings Account**. At this point we suggest you spend a little bit of time thinking about the importance of the layout of the diagram – and how this can help or hinder intended communcation.

A: Consider the class diagrams intoduced in this chapter. What conclusions do you draw about the importance of the layout of the diagram and any implications this has to either convey additional meaning, or in the worst scenario confuse and lead to assumptions being made? Either consider your own class diagram that you have developed in parallel throughout this chapter or take one of the class diagrams from this section and redraw the diagram trying an alternative layout. Solutions to this activity can be found on the Web site which accompanies this book.

In this section on class diagrams we have talked about using each refinement of the developing model to check and assess the usefulness of the model. This involves referring back to the system scope outlined in the use case diagram. A further technique for doing this can be through the use of **Class, Responsibility and Collaboration** (CRC) cards. These may or may not be familiar to you already. Whilst we do not give a detailed treatment of them in this text, some key information is provided in the *using CRC cards to explore use cases and classes* information box.

Using CRC cards to explore Use Cases and Classes	**Class, Responsibility, Collaboration** cards are a method of exploring how well a class model supports use cases. There is a card for each class. Each card has the name, the responsibilities and the collaborators of that class. They are used to role play the design and check if it is complete.

<table>
<tr><td colspan="2" align="center">Current Account</td></tr>
<tr><td>Responsibilities:

Maintains an account's balance

Allows transfers

Accumulates interest</td><td>Collaborators:

Transfer

Statement</td></tr>
</table>

Remember, the description you start from may not be complete or correct. CRC cards may open up questions which you need to take back to users and sponsors of the project. Never ignore such clues, since they usually point to a problem waiting for you in implementing or deploying the system later.

Playing the CRC card game:
- You first draw up a blank index card for each class, with just the name of that class filled in.
- You then allocate one or more cards to each person in the design team.
- Each person acts out their role, starting with the invocation of the use case by an actor
- At each step, the person holding one card takes responsibility for the next phase of the interaction.
- They either perform the required role alone or pass some of the responsibility to one or more collaborators.

Accepting responsibility corresponds to performing an operation.
Passing on part of a responsibility corresponds to sending a message.

2.2.3 Interaction Diagrams

At this point we have developed both a use case diagram and a series of increasingly detailed class diagrams. Reminder that the use case diagram helps to elaborate the requirements and the class diagram provides a static structure to support those requirements. There should, therefore, be a degree of linking between the use case and class diagrams. The UML's interaction diagrams can help us determine and check these links. What we want to examine now is how objects of the types identified in the class diagram interact to satisfy the requirements identified through the use cases. This is a key purpose of the interaction diagrams i.e. to show how objects interact in achieving some purpose.

LINK POINT	Interaction diagrams can help cross check and refine the use case and class diagrams by exploring interactions between objects to satisfy one or more use case scenarios.

UML supports two different types of interaction diagrams. These are the **sequence diagram** and the **collaboration diagram**. Both types of diagram show the objects interacting, though they have different visual presentations that may make one more suitable to a given situation – this we will see by example.

The review of the notation for interaction diagrams in Appendix A shows that conditional and iterative interactions can be included in such diagrams. However, the interaction diagrams are most helpful and clear when used to illustrate a single *scenario*. Consider what we mean by a scenario (sometimes termed a *scenario of usage* or, in the world of Extreme Programming, *user stories*) by looking again at the use case diagram in figure 2.4, specifically the use case concerning making a deposit. We know, from the use case description considered earlier, that there are alternative outcomes from this use case. Each of these represents an alternative scenario – an alternative path, if you like, through the use case. In general terms we can consider a number of successful and a number of unsuccessful outcomes, each of these being a single scenario that we could represent as an interaction diagram. The examples we will consider in this section concern interaction diagrams showing a successful deposit.

Initially we will use the sequence diagram. A sequence diagram shows the behaviour of a collection of interacting objects. The diagram is drawn in a particular manner, with the objects typically shown at the top. Each object has a dashed *lifeline* going down (or rightwards if the objects are drawn down the left-hand side of the diagram) showing its order of events. The interactions between objects are shown as messages (or signals), which are sent leaving one object's lifeline and reaching another's. Object names consist of an optional label, a colon and then the class that the object belongs to, all underlined.

The times when an object is busy can be shown by overlaying thin rectangles on its lifeline. This is an optional element of the notation and is referred to as an *activation*.

Q: *How helpful do you consider the drawing of activations to be in a particular scenario – do they add extra value in terms of clarity? This question will be addressed in the text as you read on.*

In the case of making a successful deposit, a possible collection of objects, based on the classes we found, is shown in the sequence diagram in figure 2.11. This diagram makes the point that instances of actors can also be shown if this is helpful in clarifying the scenario. Each message is represented as a labelled arrow. The labelling in this case is in a form of pseudo code – it could just as well have been named using plain text, but using a form of pseudo code can add extra information which may, or may not, be helpful in a given diagram. The use of a more structured message description can also lead to briefer and more precise message descriptions. If the class modelling phase resulted in the identification of candidate operations, then these can be referred to in the messages. Again, the point is to think carefully what you are trying to achieve through the diagram and use a clear and appropriate level of detail in the message naming.

The earlier question asked you to consider the use of activations on the sequence diagram. Perhaps this is something that you have explored already using a CASE tool such as Rational Rose. They can be helpful, and they can also get in the way at times – it again, as with many things, depends on the nature of the model. Since it is an optional element of notation, it is worth considering if your diagrams benefit from their inclusion. Their key benefit is that the return of control is implicit at the end of the activation bar. So, if you don't use them then it may be necessary to show control being returned explicitly by adding return messages to avoid confusion.

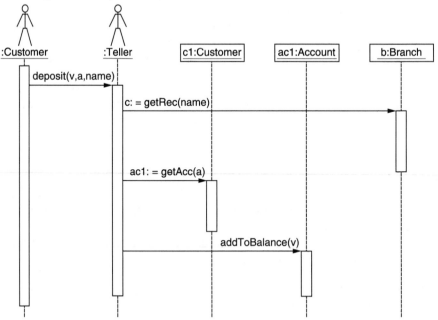

Figure 2.11: Sequence diagram showing successful deposit

Now let us consider showing the same scenario represented as a collaboration diagram. A collaboration is a collection of instances or objects which are associated with each other. The classes from which the objects are derived must have associations. To some extent, the collaboration diagram appears in a similar form to the class diagram. A key distinction, however, is that the collaboration diagram does show objects and therefore there may be multiple instances of any class present. An example diagram showing the successful deposit scenario is shown in figure 2.12.

Note that only those associations (between base class types) relevant to the current scenario need to be shown. In the example shown the additional aggregate notation is shown to further clarify the association between objects.

In comparing the diagrams in figures 2.11 and 2.12 it is quite simple to see that these represent the same scenario. A key piece of visual information that we lose in the collaboration diagram is the ordering of messages, hence the sequence numbering applied to messages in figure 2.12. The collaboration diagram has no notion of the activation bars that are available on the sequence diagram, so if it is important to show the return of control (in sequential message passing) then this must be done explicitly by the addition of a return message.

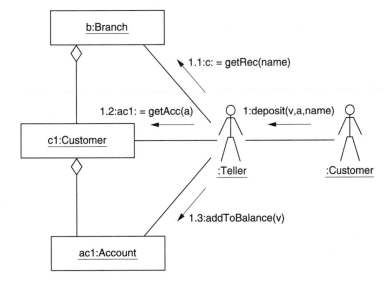

Figure 2.12: Collaboration diagram showing successful deposit

The two different variants of the interaction diagram show the same information. So, how do you choose which diagram is most suitable? Much of this will be personal choice on the part of the modeller. There are some key points that you might want to consider though. For example, the collaboration diagram tends to be more compact, so may be preferable to the sequence diagram if the scenario involves a significant number of objects. The sequence diagram can be considered more intuitive, and makes the sequence of interactions much more obvious, which may be an advantage if using the diagram to talk through a scenario with fellow modellers or clients. Whatever the deciding factor, it remains true that the two diagrams use the same core notation set, and most CASE tools will provide an automatic conversion between the two diagrams – though layout issues are left as a manual alteration by the modeller!

 A: At this point why not try taking an alternative scenario, for example, to explore what might happen in the case of an unsuccessful deposit to an account. Draw an interaction diagram to explore this scenario. Why not try both a sequence diagram and a collaboration diagram? What extra questions does this activity make you ask about the business or the system that might be required to support the business? Solutions to this activity can be found on the Web site which accompanies this book.

2.2.4 Activity Diagram

The interaction diagrams help us to examine individual scenarios. They can, however, become very complex very quickly, especially where we want to show a number of alternative outcomes. At this point we can examine the benefits of using an activity diagram. The activity diagram has many applications, for example, to examine the internal workings of a use case. They can also fulfil an important role of showing activities that transcend use case boundaries and result in dependencies. As an example of this, consider the further elaboration of the case study description that we now introduce in figure 2.13.

When a customer applies to open a new account, the teller processing the application must check with the manager. The manager has other duties though, such as checking the books from time to time.

Figure 2.13: Case study elaboration

Clearly the request for a new account depends on whether the manager is available to act in his role of authorising the customer's application. We can show such dependencies via an activity diagram, as in figure 2.14. This example diagram shows a breakdown into swimlanes of the key actors involved. Swimlanes are a simple visual aid to breaking down the areas of responsibility – they can represent instances of actors, objects or physical units of the organisation if appropriate and helpful.

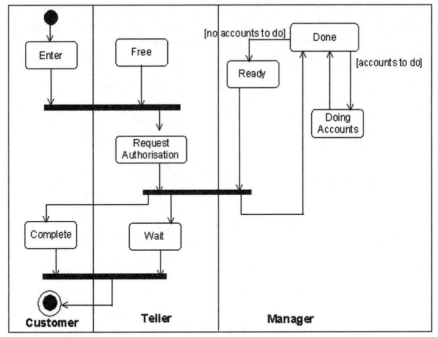

Figure 2.14: Activity diagram showing open new account

The example activity diagram illustrates clearly how this graphical representation is preferable to a simple text description, since it makes the participants' involvement in the process much clearer. This may provide stimulus for discussion and clarification that this is in fact the way things work, and is perhaps another point where the business processes may be reconsidered. This is a point we will return to again soon.

We could argue that the activity diagram in figure 2.14 observes particular states that participants need to pass through so that the process can complete (as opposed to identifying activities, though that would also be possible).

A: Have a go at redrawing the activity diagram in figure 2.14 to have named activities rather than the approach we took, which was to identify states. Is it more or less helpful to use activities or states? Is there an easy distinction between activities and states? Solutions to this activity can be found on the Web site which accompanies this book.

Observe that the **Manager** represented in a swimlane in figure 2.14 does not appear as an actor in the initial use case diagram shown in figure 2.4. It may be determined at this stage that this was an omission and a revised use case diagram prepared. A suggested possible revision is shown in the use case diagram in figure 2.15.

At this point it is worth considering whether it is *always* appropriate to go back and update the use case diagram. Would it be *wrong* not to go back and make such an update? Well, we could certainly consider that it was an omission or oversight of the initial use case diagram, but it is important to consider what benefit there is to be gained by going back and updating it. We need to consider the longer term benefits and the perceived need to maintain diagrams. The real answer depends on the project and the processes being followed with the host organisation controlling the project.

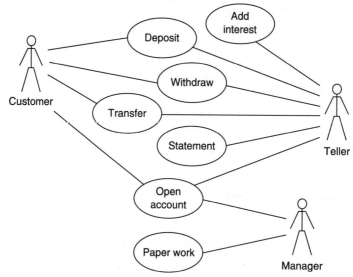

Figure 2.15: Revised use case diagram

The importance of business modelling has been referred to at various points in this chapter. Business modelling is basically about identifying the processes and rules by which a business operates. Finding a good means of modelling business processes is at the core of business modelling. The processes show the activities that need to be completed in order for the business to operate. The activities fulfil business goals, and they create and consume resources. It is important that we have an understanding of the business processes, and how they interrelate, for a number of reasons.

For example, it can be helpful to simply review existing processes to ensure a common understanding amongst employees and other interested parties (for example, customers to assure quality of work/service). In addition, if we have a good understanding of current processes it is easier to see the benefit and effect of making changes to those processes (this is referred to as *business process improvement*). Of course, if we are ultimately aiming to provide or upgrade an IT system, then that system needs to support those business processes that have been identified. In any event the need to understand and describe the business processes is paramount.

Business modelling is not a new discipline. It is part of a general view of modelling as a means of understanding and solving problems. As with software modelling, other notations exist in parallel with UML, for example the IDEF notation. However, the aim in exploring the use of UML is to continue to employ a standard notation across business and software systems modelling activities. This should improve our ability to communicate models between business modellers and IT systems modellers.

The UML standard suggests an application of variations of the core notation to model business processes, with existing UML diagrams being applied to model a different view of the business. This is summarised in the *application of core UML diagrams to Business Modelling* information box. Examples of the associated notation are presented in Appendix A.

Application of core UML diagrams to Business Modelling	**USE CASE**	can be used to describe the **business context**	
	ACTIVITY	can be used to describe **behaviour** in the business, or business **workflow**	
	CLASS	can be used to describe the **static structure** of the business	
	INTERACTION	can be used to describe **dynamic interactions** between employees and resources/things they manipulate. A series of these can indicate realisations of behaviours described in the activity diagram	

Later, in Chapter 3, we will discuss the notion of *extensions* to UML. A key form of extension that you may have heard about is the *profile*. The aim with each profile is to provide specialisations of UML notation, specifically aiming to address a particular application or problem domain without needing to revise the standard itself. What this really means is that the profile mechanism works within the rules of the existing standard to provide special characteristics.

The reason for talking about using UML for business modelling at this point is that the activity diagram can play a key role. For example, they illustrate processes and composite activities, flow between activities and conditions (indicating business rules). Numerous books and papers have developed specific approaches to this.

A: Consider attempting an activity diagram to define further business processes associated with the Bank Account case study. For example, the processes involved in establishing and setting the interest rates to be applied to the accounts held with the bank. How could an activity diagram be used to identify and name key processes and activities, highlighting essential inputs and outputs. Solutions to this activity can be found on the Web site which accompanies this book.

2.3 Summary and discussion

This chapter has used a simple case study to provide a revision of key elements of UML notation and the contexts in which it may be applied.

If you were able to follow some of our earlier suggestions, you will have developed diagrams of your own. These may have been similar or quite different to those we introduced. This brings us back to a point first raised in Chapter 1 – namely the (ir)relevance of striving for a *correct* model through the notation. We would re-emphasise the importance of developing helpful and relevant models and diagrams rather than working on the assumption that there is one single answer. A key point we continually raise in classroom-based exercises is that if the modelling activity is making you ask questions then it is in itself a beneficial exercise. It is not always about achieving an end result.

KEY POINT	The modelling activity itself is important – not just the model that you end up with.

There always seems to be particular discussion about whether to lead with use case modelling or class modelling. Our personal preference, as discussed in this chapter, is to lead with use case modelling, since it quickly allows a system scope to be defined and visualised and key actors to be recognised. These may well have to be revised at a later stage in the modelling, as in the case study we presented, but it never-the-less provides a helpful initial focus.

The reality for most modellers of course is that you are likely to do a little of both early on – a little use case modelling and a little class modelling and even some exploration of scenarios with interactions. This shows again the reality that it is infeasible to do particular design activities sequentially. What we can agree on is that, depending on our methodology, in the early stages of a project it is important to establish a clear scope and problem definition and begin to clarify requirements. To this end we should always aim to employ the most helpful techniques in the given situation, be that class and or use case modelling in the case of using UML.

A point we will continually return to concerns the importance of naming model elements (for example classes, use cases, actors etc.) and achieving a suitable physical layout. Both of these can make a big difference to the model, adding either clarity or confusion! There are some excellent texts that treat this subject in detail – though it mostly comes down to giving it some serious thought and applying an element of common sense. Check out some of the articles referred to in the further reading section in the Rational Edge online journal for some good examples.

Further reading

Although we have provided a review of UML syntax and semantics in Appendices A and B you might still feel the need for additional UML references. The following are a couple of recommendations we would make (both fairly small and relatively inexpensive texts).

Stevens, P. and Pooley, R. 2000. *Using UML: software engineering with objects and components*, Addison-Wesley. ISBN 0201648601

Fowler, M. and Scott, K. *UML Distilled: A Brief Guide to the Standard Object Modeling Language* (Object Technology Series), Addison-Wesley. ISBN 020165783X

We often find that use case modelling is an area that people feel particularly concerned about. Mostly they find it difficult to see how this can be applied successfully, mostly because the notation is so simple. While we have tried to make a case for the benefit of even simple use case diagrams, you may still be feeling sceptical. If you are one of these people, then you might find the following selection of articles helpful. It is important to make use of such articles available from the Internet. They are often much easier to read than reading a complete textbook on each subject, and they have the added advantage of being available for free!

Kurt Bittner, *Why Use Cases are Not Functions*, Rational Edge, December 2000, http://www.therationaledge.com/content/dec_00/t_ucnotfunctions.html

Ellen Gottesdiener, *Top Ten Ways Project Teams Misuse Use Cases – and How to Correct Them, Part I: Content and Style*, Rational Edge, June 2002, http://www.therationaledge.com/content/jun_02/t_misuseUseCases_eg.jsp

3

Where's the UML Going?

This chapter reviews the development of the UML notation and in doing so allows us to address the question posed by this chapter's title. This will consider what we may term *advanced features* of the UML, for example *profiles* and *extensions*. You might have heard something about these already, though they are usually topics that are only covered by the OMG UML Language Specification and white papers. We think it is important to discuss these so that you, as a UML practitioner, can begin to see which future developments might be appropriate to you.

To set the scene, we begin by providing a brief history of the evolution of the UML, then we look at how it is changing and what we can expect in the future. Whilst we accept that a history lesson can become a little boring, we think that it is important to understand at least a little about the origins of the notation, as this helps us to better understand its future direction and the people and organisations who are the driving force.

3.1 The evolution of UML

It is important to recognise that the world of OO modelling did not just begin with the UML, although you can be forgiven today for perhaps thinking that it did. There is a whole history of OO and other modelling notations that led to the development of the UML. Whilst it is not vital to know this history in depth in order to apply the UML, it is helpful in a broader sense as it explains what we see in the notation set and, arguably, some of its shortcomings.

Object orientation began as a feature within programming languages, notably SIMULA 67, which introduced the idea of classes and instances as a way of encapsulating data structures, along with inheritance as a mechanism for generalisation. This was formally referred to as *data abstraction*. In the first book to describe this approach, SIMULA BEGIN, modelling was introduced as a basis for program design. It included, as a basis for modelling, what we would clearly recognise as class and object diagrams. It could therefore be argued that the creators of SIMULA (the late Norwegian academics Kristen Nygaard and Ole-Johan Dahl) began in the sixties the developments which have led to the UML today.

Other object-oriented modelling languages began to appear between the mid-1970s and the late 1980s. The appearance and popularity of programming languages, such as Smalltalk and C++, created a need for appropriate design languages within the developing community of OO programmers. As an indicator of this, it is reported that during the period of 1989 to

1994 the number of OO modelling languages increased from less than 10 to more than 50 (http://cgi.omg.org/news/pr97/umlprimer.html). Users of the developing OO methods had trouble finding any one modelling language which met all their needs, and it was unclear how the diverse languages available could be combined. By the mid-1990s, new versions of these methods began to appear. Each began to incorporate the others' techniques along with useful views from outside the OO world, and a few clearly prominent methods emerged. Our interest at this point is what happened to a number of these, namely, Booch's methodology, Object Modelling Technique (OMT) and Object-Oriented Software Engineering (OOSE).

The development of UML itself began in late 1994 when Grady Booch and Jim Rumbaugh of Rational Software Corporation began to work on unifying their respective Booch and OMT methods. At this point they had the larger goal of a Unified Method, which would incorporate a design language within an overall methodology. In the latter part of 1995, Ivar Jacobson and his company (Objectory) joined Rational, in turn adding his OOSE method to the unification effort.

Two major contributions to the UML in the form of incorporation of pre-existing modelling views, which had been taken earlier into Booch and OMT, were:

- *sequence diagrams*, which were based on Message Sequence Charts, an international standard means of describing protocols in terms of traces of messages and which also form part of the Specification and Description Language (SDL);

- *statecharts*, which were based on David Harel's statechart notation, a self-contained, non-object oriented design approach, which had been commercialised by his i–Logix company.

As the primary authors of the Booch, OMT, and OOSE methods, Grady Booch, Jim Rumbaugh, and Ivar Jacobson were motivated to create a unified modelling language for three reasons. First, their methods were already evolving toward each other independently. It therefore made sense to continue that evolution together rather than apart, eliminating the potential for unnecessary differences that would further confuse users. Second, by unifying the semantics and notation, they could bring some stability to the object-oriented marketplace, allowing projects to settle on one mature modelling language. This stability would allow tool builders to focus on delivering more useful features, which would enhance the uptake of the unified notation. Third, they expected that their collaboration would yield improvements over all three earlier methods, helping them to capture lessons learned and to address problems that none of their methods previously handled well.

The efforts of Booch, Rumbaugh, and Jacobson resulted in the release of the UML 0.9 and 0.91 documents in June and October of 1996. They were now aware that even a unified language was a huge undertaking and at this point postponed any effort at an over-arching methodology. During 1996, the UML authors invited and received feedback from the general community. They incorporated this feedback, but it was clear that additional focused attention was still required.

The work so far was being driven by efforts at Rational. In early 1995, Ivar Jacobson (then Chief Technology Officer of Objectory) and Richard Soley (then Chief Technology Officer of the Object Management Group (OMG)) decided to push harder to achieve standardisation in the methods marketplace. In June 1995, the OMG hosted a meeting of major methodologists. This resulted in the first worldwide agreement to seek methodology standards, under the sponsorship of the OMG.

During 1996, it became clear that several organisations saw the UML as strategic to their business. A Request for Proposal (RFP) issued by OMG provided the catalyst for these organisations to join forces and produce a joint RFP response. A UML Partners consortium was established, with several organisations contributing towards a strong UML 1.0 definition. Those acknowledged as contributing most to the UML 1.0 definition include: Digital Equipment Corporation, Hewlett-Packard, i-Logix, IntelliCorp, IBM, ICON Computing, MCI Systemhouse, Microsoft, Oracle, Rational Software, TI, and Unisys. This collaboration produced UML 1.0, which was submitted to the OMG in January 1997 as an initial RFP response.

Also at this time other contributors (ObjecTime, Platinum Technology, Ptech, Taskon, Reich Technologies and Softeam) submitted separate RFP responses to the OMG. These companies joined the UML partners to contribute their ideas, and together the partners produced the revised UML 1.1 response. The focus of the UML 1.1 release was to improve the clarity of the UML 1.0 semantics and to incorporate contributions from the new partners. It was submitted to the OMG for their consideration and adopted in late 1997.

Another significant outside contribution at around this time was the creation of a standard from for writing constraints in the UML. For those seeking genuinely sound semantics for the notation, it was vital that such a formal language be an optional part of any models. This resulted in the object constraint language (OCL) becoming part of the UML, based in large part on the ideas of Steve Cook and John Daniels.

Since then the OMG, which is owned by the community, not by one commercial interest, have owned the rights to the UML (relinquished by Rational). This enables the OMG to orchestrate the development of the UML further, and make such information publicly available. The development of further versions of the UML standard are a result of the combined efforts of an OMG committee, which includes representatives of various companies including Rational (now owned by IBM), who maintain a keen interest in developments.

Further updates to the standard have had a number of objectives. For example, cleaning up problems with the internal UML meta-model, clarifying ambiguities in the original document, improving naming consistency and addressing features required by specialised areas and domains. Specific developments that you should be aware of are discussed in the following section. Each area is typically driven forward by a task force, which prepares proposals for ratification and incorporation within the overall UML standard. One key area as the UML stabilises is inter-operability of tools, which has led to a standard, defined in XML, known as XMI. All UML tools are adopting this as their model exchange format.

3.2 Advanced features of UML

This section considers features that we have loosely labelled as *advanced*. They are advanced in as much as they are not typically the first things that you learn about when you first come across the UML. They are areas that you tend to become aware of as your knowledge and experience with the UML develops.

The first of these concerns an understanding of the extension mechanisms that already exist in the UML. The other three have been developed as the UML matures and have come through the notation review process (more on that later). These key features, *Object Constraint Language* (OCL), *Action Semantics* and *Profiles,* aim to add to the expressiveness of UML

3.2.1 Extension Mechanisms

There are three basic mechanisms that already exist within the UML that allow the modeller to add extra clarification to the model being developed. You will have encountered some or all of these mechanisms already; *stereotypes, tagged values,* and *constraints*. These extension mechanisms allow an enrichment of both the static and dynamic model elements, creating means of expression that are unknown to the UML. They also form the basis of domain specific inter-working of tools, discussed below under profiles.

Stereotypes are the most common mechanism that you may have already seen. Stereotypes are included in the double chevron braces, for example «uses» or «extends» and «interface». A number of stereotypes are already defined in the UML language, but modellers can define additional ones as required. A stereotype defines a more specialised form of a basic element of UML. Both *class* and *actor* are, thus, stereotypes of the basic element, *classifier*. In the case of actor, a new icon is used, which is an alternative way of showing a stereotype within the notation. We will look at stereotypes in more detail when we use deployment diagrams.

Tag definitions comprise, as the name implies, both a tag's name and its type. They are used to add named attributes to an existing UML element type when a stereotype is defined. Tagged values can then be used to specify a constraint on either a stereotype or an instance of an element, including a stereotype. Most standard UML model elements have predefined tags, which you can discover in the UML Semantics definition document.

Constraints are provided as a mechanism that defines limits (i.e. constraints) on a model element, especially its tags. These may be defined using free format text, but increasingly they are expressed more formally using the Object Constraint Language (OCL). Constraints are enclosed in curly braces, for example {amount is multiple of £10.00} may be a constraint against an attribute or a tag in a class.

Figure 3.1 shows the definition of a new stereotype, Persistent, which is a specialisation of Class, using tag definitions and constraints. Any instance of Persistent will have to give values to these tags, while respecting the constraint.

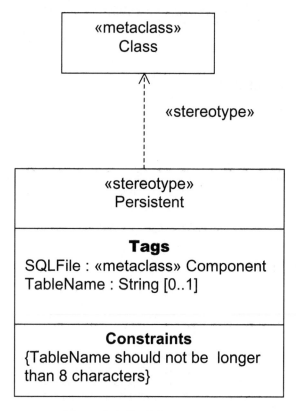

Figure 3.1: Defining a stereotype

3.2.2 Object Constraint Language

OCL has been part of UML since its beginning (well, since UML 1.1 anyway). It allows the modeller to express conditions on an invocation in a formally defined way. Amongst other things this allows the expression of invariants, pre-conditions, post-conditions and whether an object reference is allowed to be null.

The formalising of constraints is important for many modelling exercises, but most importantly for applications concerning safety or mission critical systems. The more we move down the route of formalising UML the more we can carry out verification and validation activities against a model. The end result is that we have greater confidence in the model. The increased formality is also important for the purposes of tool support. This helps because we can begin to consider wider automatic verification and validation checks. It is also important though in supporting other areas where tools can help, for example model conversion (between diagram types or notations other than UML) and code generation.

On the other hand, we are often working less formally and may choose to express our constraints accordingly. As usual, we should not be worried about providing detail and precision which we are not sure of.

3.2.3 Action Semantics

Action semantics is considered an extension to the UML and was introduced in UML 1.5. The aim of this extension is to support the expression of actions as UML objects. An action object may take a set of inputs and transform it into a set of outputs (although one or both sets may be empty), or may change the state of the system, or both. Actions may be chained, with one action's outputs being another action's inputs. Actions are assumed to occur independently – that is, there is infinite concurrency in the system, unless you chain them or specify this in another way. This concurrency model is a natural fit to the distributed execution environment of modern enterprise and Internet applications.

3.2.4 UML Profiles

The concept of profiles has been around the UML for sometime. Consider the following definition taken from the UML version 1.3 specification document.

> A UML Profile is a predefined set of Stereotypes, Tagged Values, Constraints and notation icons that collectively specialise and tailor the UML for a specific domain or process (e.g. Unified Process profile). A profile does not extend UML by adding any new basic concepts. Instead it provides conventions for applying and specialising standard UML to a particular environment or domain.

UML Profile Definition

Profiles are an accepted means of extending the UML notation to specific application and problem domains. One of the most important developments introduced in UML 1.4 was the set of guidelines for writing profiles. The aim of the profile concept is to allow communities of users to tailor the language to particular areas of application. The point being that the UML itself does not have to change to support these application domains – the profile makes use of existing UML constructs.

We can regard each profile as defining a domain specific interpretation of the UML. There are a number of expected applications for such profiles, for example:

Technology and Language Mappings: Every technical target for implementation (e.g. programming language, database or middleware) is a potential candidate for defining a dedicated UML profile.

General Technical Domains: Profiles for Enterprise Distributed Object Computing (EDOC) and real-time domains already exist through the OMG. Other candidate domains are business modelling and workflow.

Specific Application Domains: This would suggest profiles to support specific domains, such as finance or manufacturing. Profiles to support geographical systems would also come under this category.

Modelling Software Development Processes: Profiles might be defined and applied to support the use of parts of the UML to support different stages of the development lifecycle.

This still leaves the question of *what a profile is* unanswered. To move towards a more concrete understanding, a UML profile is a specification that does one or more of the following.

General Definition of a UML Profile	Identifies a subset of the UML metamodel
	Specifies well-formedness rules beyond those specified by the identified subset of the UML metamodel. Well-formedness rule is a term used in the normative UML metamodel specification (ad/97-08-04) to describe a set of constraints written in UML's Object Constraint Language (OCL) that contributes to the definition of a metamodel element
	Specifies standard elements beyond those specified by the identified subset of the UML metamodel. Standard element is a term used in the UML metamodel specification to describe a standard instance of a UML stereotype, tagged value or constraint
	Specifies semantics, expressed in natural language, beyond those specified by the identified subset of the UML metamodel
	Specifies common model elements, expressed in terms of the profile

The definition in the above table may appear to be written in a form of legalese. Such, unfortunately, is the nature of specification documents that aim for clarity and formality. The definition basically says that a profile is a combination of a set of notation, extension mechanisms, particular icons/symbols and semantic descriptions of how they might be applied. The following summarises profiles that have already been developed:

UML for Data Modelling	Defines modelling constructs specifically aiming to model databases and database components.
UML for Web Modelling	Defines constructs to model components of Web-based architectures; e.g. architectures, Web pages, forms and frames.
UML for Business Modelling	Defines adaptations to core UML notation sets (use case, class, activity and interaction diagrams) to focus on business modelling.
UML for Realtime Modelling	Defines constructs for modelling realtime issues i.e. representing time and time related interactions. Main focus concerns adaptations to class and collaboration diagrams.
UML Profile for Schedulability, Performance and Time	Defines constructs and stereotypes to support broad range of time critical modelling problems.
UML Profile for CORBA®	Provides a standard means for expressing the semantics of CORBA IDL using UML notation and support for expressing these semantics with UML tools.
UML Profile for Enterprise Application Integration (EAI)	Provides a metadata interchange standard for information about accessing application interfaces. The goal is to simplify application integration by standardising application metadata for invoking and translating application information.
UML Profile for Enterprise Distributed Object Computing (EDOC)	The vision of the EDOC Profile is to simplify the development of component-based EDOC systems by means of a modelling framework, based on UML 1.4 and conforming to the OMG Model Driven Architecture.

Note that there is a distinction in the above between those titled "*UML for*" and "*UML Profile for*". The latter are proposals that are being worked through by the OMG (those above have been taken from the OMG Web site). The former are proposed by the Rational Corporation (now under ownership of IBM). The origin or official status of a profile does not necessarily make it any better or worse, and we would encourage you to explore any of the above that look relevant to your purposes.

References for further reading on some of the above profiles can be found at the end of this chapter. The majority of these references are white papers and documents available freely from the Internet.

3.3 Future developments

In mid-2001 OMG members started work on a major upgrade. That proposed upgrade will lead to UML 2.0. The following are the four separate areas of work that are associated with these developments:

- UML Infrastructure
- UML Superstructure
- Object Constraint Language
- UML Diagram Interchange

Whilst it is important and interesting to keep an eye on future developments, the implications of UML 2.0 are expected to be minimal to the average UML practitioner. The main focus in the above subject areas is a major tidying exercise of the UML standard itself – not a revision of the supported notation set.

If you are an OMG member then you can follow the adoption process for 2.0 in detail, and influence it as well, by following the links on the OMG Web site. Alas, non-members can only view the RFPs (requirements documents for each process) – though in themselves they are still quite interesting and informative.

3.4 Summary

The main aim of this chapter has been to show you that the UML has both an established history and a future. The UML is a living language, and its immediate future is being driven through the management of the OMG, which continues to have considerable input from industry and research organisations.

The various contributors see a need to keep developing the standard, and hopefully making the notation better by increments. We would hope that some of these modifications involve a rationalisation process rather than just adding more and more to the standard. Time will tell.

Having acknowledged areas of recent development, in particular the development of profiles, we would encourage you to continue to work through the material in this book. The case studies in particular make reference to a number of the profiles and we will return to consider their merits in Chapter 9. Keep in mind that whilst it is good to be aware of future directions of the UML's development, it is more important to develop a strong command of the core notation. Our own view is that many modelling problems can be expressed and resolved with the core notation as it currently stands, and as a UML practitioner that should be your main focus. Once you have such an understanding you are better placed to judge the added benefit of adopting a particular profile.

Further reading

Many of the related readings are in the form of white papers available via the Web. Textbooks are also in development that will expand on these profiles, but many have yet to emerge – in the meantime a bit of freely available material is probably welcome.

The following are a selection of interesting reads available in the form of white papers:

> *Requirements for UML Profiles*, Analysis and Design Platform Task Force, Version 1.0, December 1999, OMG Document ad/99-12-32.

> Jim Rumbaugh, *Trends in UML and eDevelopment*, The Rational Edge, December 2000, http://www.therationaledge.com/content/dec_00/f_uml.html

Since we find it healthy to consider opposing views, you might like to explore the following article that considers why UML profiles are surplus to requirement:

> Desmond D'Souza, Aamod Sane and Alan Birchenough, *UML Profiles Considered Redundant, 1999*,
> http://cgi.omg.org/pub/umlrtf/UML_Profiles_Considered_Redundant.pdf

For white papers and other documentation regarding the UML profiles proposed by Rational (and therefore supported by their Rose and RUP suite of tools), check out the Rational UML Resource http://www.rational.com/uml/resources/.

For details of the UML profiles proposed by the OMG, check out the OMG Web site http://www.omg.org/technology/uml/.

4

The Importance of Process

This is the final chapter in Part One, and it aims to put a number of key issues regarding process in context before we move on to Part Two and become involved in a myriad of case studies and diagram types. We have included this chapter here on the assumption that many people will read this book in sequence (perhaps a large assumption). We wanted people to consider the importance of, and what is meant by, process before moving into the case study chapters. This will set the scene for what we return to in Part Three.

Our concern here is to raise the profile of the *ways in which people work* and our aim is to make the point that *process is important*. What do we mean by this? Well, taking a very broad and simple view, people tend to adopt a variety of means to tackle problems and situations in their everyday lives. We all do it all the time – often unconsciously or as a result of habits and patterns of behaviour that we adopt. Depending on the size and nature of the problem that we are undertaking, we may choose to use different approaches in different situations. This is a healthy approach, as we rarely find that one approach will be suitable for all types of problems. These approaches may be informal and mostly kept in our heads, or they may be more formal in that they are written down – at least to some extent. When you are working with other people, for example, as part of a collaborative team or when you are trying to demonstrate to someone the rigour and therefore quality of your work, it is increasingly important to be clear and open about the means you employ to tackle problems. So, under such circumstances our approach to tackling problems needs to be clarified and formalised. This is considered to be good practice in the IT and many other professions.

These *means to tackle problems* are what we more formally refer to as processes, methods and/or methodologies. They describe the structure of the approach we will undertake to solve a problem. In the IT profession, examples of problems that we can identify may be requirements elicitation, business process improvement, software development, testing and evaluation. We are going to look at how you might approach such problems in a consistent and effective manner and why it is important to do so. Unlike many other authors, we are not going to do this by giving you our own (or favourite) process/methodology. We prefer to look at what it is that you *need* in order to carry out your tasks and to suggest *how* to identify an appropriate approach that may help you.

There are numerous reasons for using a particular method, the majority of which should be to the advantage of those using it. Unfortunately, for reasons that we'll discuss, this is not always the case. A key issue in looking at alternative approaches is finding an appropriate means to compare them. How can you decide on the appropriateness of one process over another? This is a common problem, and one that we discuss further in Part Three, where we provide a comparison of a number of common methodologies using a framework based on the Capability Maturity Model (CMM) for Software. In this chapter we have a section that discusses a number of common and widely differing processes. The purpose of including them in this chapter is not to provide a detailed introduction to each of them, rather it aims to reinforce for you the range of alternatives that are out there. This in itself is a healthy activity once in a while, and it also helps to see the importance of finding an appropriate way to make comparisons – because at first glance it may seem like an impossible task, but we'll return to talk about that more in Part Three.

You will have seen already that we are intermixing a range of terminology – *process*, *method* and *methodology*. The term methodology needs a little more attention, and this is something that we will discuss in the next section, since the use of this term causes some confusion (and more than a few arguments amongst academics).

4.1   About that word *methodology*

The term methodology is often used in connection with defined and formal approaches to problem solving. Before carrying on with this chapter, we want to spend a little bit of time talking about what is meant when we use this term, and hopefully to resolve some of the confusion (and arguments) that arise in its use. Well, we are never actually going to resolve many of these arguments, but we can at least tell you what we think on the subject.

In order to discuss this we need to have at least a working definition, so we'll begin here by considering a number.

The word *methodology* literally means the *study of methods*. Picking up any dictionary will provide you with a slightly more elaborate definition. For example, consider the following quote, taken from the Oxford Dictionary, which defines a methodology as the "*study of systematic methods of scientific research*".

However, the term has been adopted by the computing and IT communities where it means something more akin to a *method* or *process*. Consider a definition suggested by Peter Checkland. Peter is a leading author in the area of systems thinking and its relation to real-world problem solving, especially connected to the creation of information systems (we've included a reference to one of his key revised publications in the *Further reading* section of this chapter). Consider the following *definition of methodology* information box, which shows Peter's thoughts on the subject.

Definition of methodology	"A methodology will lack the precision of a technique but will be a firmer guide to action than a philosophy. Where a technique tells you how and a philosophy tells you what, a methodology will contain elements of both what and how." (Checkland 1981)

Let us consider here for a moment how language is a wonderful and expressive means of communication. Let us also consider that it can get us into a number of terrible fixes at times. Please note that this is, of course, a very good example of why we explore the use of graphical notations such as UML to help us describe a problem and simplify the words involved. Language can often get in our way, especially where we have a choice between many words that we may use to mean the same thing. Consider the specific examples in the following *words that are often used interchangeably* information box.

Words that are often used interchangeably	technique tool notation
	methodology method process

With reference to the words in the above information box, UML is our technique, tool or notation – it is the *thing* that we will be using – that's principally what UML is. The term tool is perhaps a little unexpected, as we increasingly assume that a tool is necessarily computer-based. In a broader context, other techniques may apply which may be graphical or textual. We have already noted, in Chapter 2, that whilst UML provides a graphical notation and the associated benefits, there is still a place for other techniques (for example, text) to supplement our modelling efforts.

What we need then is an approach that describes *how we will use UML*. This is where the methodology, method or process comes in. We believe that the terms methodology, method and process may be used interchangeably with little loss of point or meaning. You will come across many individuals and text books that will make great and significant points about the correct terminology to use and the misuse of the English language in mixing the use of these three terms. Whilst we do not wish to either belittle them or deny that the use of language is important, our emphasis here is on understanding – and why, irrespective of the term used, we care about these ideas at all. We are not going to become distracted by either the use or misuse of the term methodology. What we are concerned with is identifying an agreed way of working in order to find a solution to a problem.

We have frequently found it helpful to consider the description of a process or methodology as a framework. So, in a practical sense, what is it that we help to achieve through the use of such a framework? The point is that it defines a way of working, giving us the scaffolding to support a project, by defining the contributions shown in the *key contributions of a process* information box on the following page.

This then gives us a working understanding of what a process has to offer, and why it is important to consider the adoption of one to support our working. You might be thinking at this point that we don't really need to structure or formalise something that seems such common sense. Well, the real problem comes when you are working as a team, and, let's be honest, very few people work entirely on their own. Even if you are working *by yourself*, it is rare that you are working *for yourself* i.e. there are other people involved, for example customers! The process or methodology is a means to help people realise an end goal – as we said at the outset of this chapter, it is an approach to solving a problem.

Key contributions of a process	**SCOPE**	the scope of the project lifecycle
	STRUCTURE	the number of stages or phases to break the work down and their relationship to one another
	ARTEFACTS	a number of key deliverables to be produced through the stages or phases
	ITERATIONS	the importance and number of iterations envisaged
	TECHNIQUES	identification of appropriate techniques that can help at each stage of the project. For example, the use of notations or tool support

No process or methodology is a precise mechanism – you cannot just crank the handle and have the result pop out at the end. This is a mistake people often make when trying to use a process, setting their expectations of the process itself too high. The choice and application of methodology is very important, which is why we have dedicated so much of this book to this discussion – in this chapter and again in Part Three.

To take this discussion further, the following section introduces some common process models and methodologies, three of which we will return to discuss further in Part Three of this book.

4.2   Examples of processes

This section does not aim to provide an introduction in detail to specific processes. However, in order to put this chapter in some firmer context, we think it is helpful at this point to introduce a number of processes or methodologies that you may have heard of, or may indeed have experience with. In the following names and descriptions you will again see a variety of choices of term – some choose to talk about process and some methodology. Hopefully the previous section has dispelled some of the confusion in use of different terms.

What you will also see by looking at these examples is the wide spectrum of processes that exist. We could argue there is one to serve all types of different problems, project sizes and ways of working that people would care to adopt, but we won't. Use this section to consider the broad selection of options available, understand some of the different ways in which these processes came into being and think a little further about how you could begin to make a choice about which would be suitable for your own use under certain conditions.

Additional references to each of the following can be found in the *Further reading* section of this chapter.

Structured Systems Analysis and Design Methodology (SSADM)	SSADM was commissioned by the CCTA (Central Computing and Telecommunications Agency) in a bid to standardise the varied IT projects being developed across government departments. It has been in use since 1981, and Version 4 was launched in 1990. SSADM is an open standard, and revolves around the use of three key techniques, namely Logical Data Modelling, Data Flow Modelling and Entity/Event Modelling. SSADM consists of five main modules, which are in turn broken down into a complex hierarchy of stages, steps and tasks. The SSADM presents itself as a highly structured process model with a clear set of recognised deliverables.
Rational Unified Process (RUP)	The RUP is a product of the Rational Corporation (the same organisation behind the formation of the UML itself, as discussed in Chapter 3). RUP has been around since the late 1980s, and presents a highly structured process model, advocating key workflows and phases. Iterations within phases are defined, with key deliverables suggested. Full tool support for the RUP is available (via Rational Product Suite).
Waterfall	The Waterfall method goes way back in computing history. (Before that it emerged in production engineering.) It abstracts the essential activities of software development and lists them in their most primitive sequence of dependency. The waterfall concept captures the flow from one stage in the system lifecycle to the next. The verbs of waterfall development are "analyse", "design", "code" and "test". Real development projects (software and other) rarely follow the Waterfall model literally, mostly because the model can and is applied to itself recursively, the number of recursions depend on the particular project. Compared to the RUP or SSADM the Waterfall model describes a more conceptual approach to work management rather than presenting a structured description of work. Simple problems lend well to simple Waterfall approximations.
Soft Systems Methodology (SSM)	The SSM approach is grounded in the research work of Peter Checkland at Lancaster University. It emphasises the importance of the role played by people in the project and their eventual role in using any system that is developed. A defined structure, set of goals, tools and techniques are themselves inadequate, and do not consider the implications of concepts, culture and language. The SSM approach is necessarily fuzzier and less structured than the RUP or SSADM – SSM itself claims to be broader than such typical methodologies. The central aim is to determine a view (or views) which forms the basis of the system requirements.
Object-oriented Process, Environment and Notation (OPEN)	OPEN was developed (and is maintained) by members of the OPEN Consortium. OPEN is a public domain, fully object-oriented methodology/process. It aims to encapsulate business issues, quality issues, modelling issues and reuse issues within its end-to-end lifecycle support for software development. Flexibility is a key focus of the OPEN approach. Its metamodel-based framework can be tailored to individual domains or projects taking into account personal skills, organizational culture and requirements peculiar to

each industry domain. The process defines a core matrix which is used to map Activities of the lifecycle and Tasks which are the smallest unit of work. A second matrix then links the Task (the statement of goals i.e. the "what") to the Techniques (the way the goal can be achieved i.e. the "how").

Catalysis

The original developers of Catalysis are Desmond D'Souza and Alan Wills, who co-authored the first Catalysis book. More of a philosophy than a structured method. Catalysis is an approach for the systematic business-driven development of component-based systems based around the use of UML. It has been applied since 1992. Catalysis is a non-proprietary method, in use in many projects, and supported by tools and related products and services from several companies.

Rapid Application Development (RAD)

RAD is a term currently used in association with a whole range of tools, techniques, methods, and even information systems management styles. The RAD term is credited to James Martin, who published a book with the same title. Martin defines the key objectives as high quality systems, fast development and delivery, and low costs.

In 1992, a number of experienced RAD developers came together and decided to develop a new methodology, to combine the best elements of existing methods and practical experience. The result was the Dynamic System Development Method (DSDM). In 1995 the DSDM consortium was founded in Benelux.

Extreme Programming (XP)

XP claims a refreshing new approach, emphasising customer involvement and promoting team work. The rules and practices employed must support each other. There is an XP Map which shows how rules and practices come together to form a development methodology. Unproductive activities are trimmed to reduce costs and frustration. Managers, customers, and developers are all part of a team dedicated to delivering quality software. XP claims to improve a software project in five essential ways; communication, simplicity, rules, feedback, and courage. XP programmers communicate with their customers and fellow programmers. They keep their design simple and clean. They get feedback by testing their software starting on day one. They deliver the system to the customers as early as possible and implement changes as suggested.

Having considered a number of examples, the following section considers the reasons why we would want to use a particular methodology. As sensible as this seems, it is something that people often do not do. Or perhaps, even worse, they don't think that it matters – isn't one processor methodology very much like any other?

 Q: *What is the purpose of adopting (and perhaps adapting) an existing process? Why not make one up of your own devising? This question will be addressed in the text as you read on.*

4.3   Reasons for using an established approach

A key aim of this chapter is to break away from the myth and mystery surrounding the term methodology and get to the practical root of the problem. Keep reminding yourself that a process or methodology is a way of formalising common sense and best practice.

KEY POINT	a process, method or methodology is a way of formalising common sense and best practice

There are a number of benefits of using existing processes and methodologies. The key ones that we would like to highlight are summarised in the *benefits of using an established approach* information box and are discussed further in the text that follows.

Benefits of using an established approach	A recommended approach to tackling a problem
	Helps support project planning efforts
	Essential framework for team working
	Common understanding of typical project lifecycle

The following expand further on the benefits of using an established approach outlined above:

A recommended approach to tackling a problem

A methodology puts structure on what might otherwise be chaos. A structure or framework is a key contribution that a methodology makes. A methodology is an approach that has been predefined, so in principle we are learning from the experience of others – why reinvent the wheel and create a new methodology when others have already done the work?

Helps support project planning efforts

A framework immediately starts to support the project planning activity by identifying key stages, phases, deliverables etc.

Essential framework for team working

A framework is important for people working individually, but it is essential for people working as a team to support communication and avoid unnecessary confusion and misunderstanding.

Common understanding of typical project lifecycle

A methodology can unify the activities across a project from inception through, where applicable, to the implementation and ongoing maintenance of an IT system. This encompasses the activities of business and software systems modelling.

It is not difficult to see the benefits to be gained by adopting an *agreed* methodology. The problems really begin when we start to look at which methodology to adopt. This is not actually as complex as it seems, and that is the subject of the following section.

Q: *Considering the benefits of using an established process outlined in this section, does it really matter which one we choose? In principle isn't any process better than none? This question will be addressed in the text as you read on.*

4.4   The importance of making an appropriate choice

There are as many reasons for choosing a particular process or methodologies as there are choices (possibly more so). Based on our experience, some of the main *influencing factors* are summarised in the following information box.

Influencing factors	Company doctrine
	Customer influence
	Standards development/application
	Personal bias/belief
	Training/experience

The following expand further on the influencing factors outlined above:

Company doctrine

an organisation may have a policy that determines a commitment to use a particular methodology. The policy may be a standard one in the public domain, or may often be a company's own variation. This typically tends to be the case where a company has a level of quality assurance and certification to maintain, for example ISO9000, TickIT or CMM.

Customer influence

a customer may determine, as part of a project contract agreement that a particular methodology be adopted. This may be particularly relevant where the customer organisation has a particular quality level to maintain in its work as mentioned above re CMM or ISO9000 certification.

Standards development /application

the adoption of particular standards with an organisation or project may influence the methodology chosen. For example, many organisations that use UML automatically adopt the Rational Unified Process (RUP).

Personal bias/belief	the personal contribution/experiences of team members may influence the chosen methodology with an organisation across all projects or within a particular project. They may simply advocate adopting what they have used previously since it is familiar.
Training/experience	a particular methodology may be adopted in order to try it out and evaluate it. This may be a good idea if participants are experienced and the project is low risk. It may be most suitable to do in the context of internal company projects.
Modellers right to choose	this concerns the benefit to be gained in allowing the modellers to have input to determine the chosen way of working. No methodology will work without the support and buy-in from the practitioners.

The above are all factors that may well influence the adoption of one or other processes within an organisation or project team. Note that nothing in the above seems to take into account the particular characteristics of the problem to be solved and the appropriateness of the chosen methodology. If the above factors are the only ones we take into account then we are perhaps in trouble. We need to think things through a little more carefully than this. This is a point we will discuss further in Part Three of this book.

An inappropriate process can be a distraction and do actual damage, especially when working as a team. Are all stages, deliverables etc. of a given methodology applicable to each instance in which the methodology is applied? Since this is doubtful, it is important to maintain an element of flexibility and choice. If we are blindly carrying out stages of a process and producing deliverables without ever asking about the *relevance* of what we are doing, then we are not working either smartly or professionally. We are at best wasting time and effort, and at worst we may miss something vital in the process.

KEY POINT	The chosen methodology needs to reflect the particular problem as well as the people who will be applying it.

4.5 Summary and discussion

This chapter has discussed the need for a methodology. We have discussed common confusion over terminology being used – when do we talk about *methodology*, *method* or *process*? For the purposes of this text we accept that these terms can be used interchangeably – this is the reality for most people.

The process helps to define the scope, structure, artefacts, iterations and techniques to help on a particular project. It is important that any given process be applied intelligently – by this we mean consider whether a process needs tailoring and adapting to a particular project or set of circumstances.

This chapter introduced a range of example processes and their characteristics. The aim in introducing them was to make a point about the diversity of processes available, and the further importance of making sure that attention is given to making an appropriate choice. While we examined approaches and reasons for comparing methodologies, the key concept of iterations shone through as being of prime importance. This is acknowledging that we only make progress through increments and revisions. Specifically, it emphasises the asking of questions at each stage, and revision of previous ideas/work as appropriate. It is important to accept that initial models will have weaknesses that can be strengthened by iteration and revision.

As we said at the outset of this chapter, we do not advocate the use of any specific methodology throughout this book, but a key factor in any process is the concept of progress through iterations. This is something that we strongly emphasise throughout the text. Accepting that we won't get close to an acceptable model in a single pass is key to any modelling exercise. We need to accept that the only way to reach a more appropriate model is by going through each step a number of times. The number of iterations necessary is a matter for project planning and requires judgement on the part of the modellers and associated project participants to know when they have something of a suitable quality to work with.

Further reading

The following are a selection of further readings based on material discussed in this chapter which consider general issues of process methods and problem solving.

Checkland, P., *Systems Thinking, Systems Practice: Includes a 30-year Retrospective*, John Wiley and Sons Ltd, 1999, ISBN 0471986062

Avison, D.E. and Fitzgerald, G., *Where now for development methodologies?* Communications of the ACM, January 2003, Volume 46 Issue 1, pp78–82, 2003

The following are particular readings concerning the processes discussed in section 4.2. Some of these are text books, but some introductory material is also available in the form of white papers via the Internet.

For the OPEN process, consider the following reading material:

Graham, I., Henderson-Sellers, B. and Younessi, H., *The OPEN Process Specification*, Addison-Wesley, 1997, ISBN 0201331330.

Henderson-Sellers, B., *OPEN: toward method convergence?*, Object Magazine (Nov 1996), 6(9), 56–59. Available from http://www.markv.com/OPEN/

SSADM continues to be developed by the Office of Government Commerce (OGC). For further information on official SSADM publication refer to their Web site at http://www.ogc.gov.uk/. For a bit of a lighter read you might like to consider the following:

> Downs, E., Clare, P. and Coe, I., *Structured systems analysis and design method: application and context*, second edition, Prentice Hall International (UK) Ltd. Hertfordshire, 1988, ISBN 0-13-853698-8

Original discussion of Waterfall process can be found in:

> Royce, W.W., *Managing the Development of Large Software Systems*, IEEE 1970

The principal Web site for further information concerning Extreme Programming is available via http://www.extremeprogramming.org/. The Web site is very helpful and contains lots of supplementary information and contacts. In addition you might like to consider the following text book:

> Beck, K., *Extreme Programming Explained, Embrace Change*, Addison-Wesley, Addison-Wesley Pub C, 2000, ISBN 0201616416

For Catalysis, the main Web site is available via http://www.catalysis.org/. This Web site offers a wide range of material and publications and links to support for training and tools. There is of course, the core text book on Catalysis by D'Souza and Wills. The text material for this book is able available from the Catalysis Web site (shown in the following URL).

> D'Souza, D.F. and Wills, A.C., *Objects, Components, and Frameworks With UML: The Catalysis Approach*, Addison-Wesley Object Technology Series, ISBN 0201310120, http://www.catalysis.org/books/ocf/index.htm

The following are two RAD related publications. The first is the seminal text on the RAD process. The latter is a current text looking at DSDM, the close relative of the RAD approach:

> Martin, J., *Rapid Application Development*, Macmillan USA, ISBN 0023767758, 1999

> Stapleton, J., DSDM: *Dynamic Systems Development Method: The Method in Practice*, Addison Wesley, ISBN 0201178893, 2003

For SSM, a helpful resource is http://members.tripod.com/SSM_Delphi/ssm4.html with further information being found in the texts shown below:

> Checkland, P. and Holwell, S. *Information, Systems and Information Systems: making sense of the field*, Wiley, 1998, ISBN 0471958204

Part Two

Case Studies

5

The Trusty Car Company

In this chapter we are going to look at applying UML to examine the problems encountered by an organisation and its business operations. The focus for the case study is a car sales company called the Trusty Car Company (TCC). Like the Bank Account case study in Chapter 2, the subject material in this chapter is itself fictitious. However, it contains many issues and questions that are raised in comparable studies of real organisations, and this helps us to discuss a number of related concerns regarding the application of UML. This is a case study that we have a lot of experience in using in a variety of courses (both for academia and industry) and it always seems to work rather well. We hope that this will also be your experience as you begin to work through Part Two of this book.

The choice of context for such a case study is important. It is anticipated that the majority of readers will have encountered such a business as a customer and so will have some appreciation of the business context. This reasoning is similar to that used in Chapter 2, where we assume that the majority of people have some experience of banks and bank accounts. This does not mean that you know everything there is to know about such a business context, but that you have some understanding on which to work and this makes the subject material reasonably comfortable. Of the four case studies included, we consider this one to be a good introduction to this part of the book. We shall deal with the case study itself in subsequent sections. Before doing so, it is important to gain a sense of the importance of this type of case study and why we have included it in this book. The purpose here is to focus more on the application of UML to model the problems associated with a particular business. The initial business modelling activity will endeavour to capture these concerns, and we shall see how these issues follow through into software design. Through this we will illustrate and examine the role played by activity diagrams, use cases, class diagrams and data modelling aspects of UML. These points are summarised in the following *UML Used in this Chapter* information box.

UML Used in this Chaper	**USE CASE DIAGRAM**	to examine and capture requirements of the business and therefore of some system that may potentially support the business.
	CLASS DIAGRAM	to start to examine system structure.
	INTERACTION DIAGRAM	to express system dynamics.
	ACTIVITY DIAGRAM	to illustrate dependencies in system.

5.1 Case study introduction

Preliminary analysis has shown that the garages are having trouble keeping track of stock within the group, and communication is not all that it could be. Particularly, the record of the group's network of new and used vehicles on stock at any time is frequently out of date, if in fact it can be found at all. This stock record is currently just a paper-based number of faxed lists that are circulated around on a weekly basis. Consequently, this can frequently be out of date, and sales staff resort to constant telephone calls to check current availability to avoid customer disappointment. The garages in the TCC group wish to improve this aspect of their business. They perceive that this will help them to improve efficiency and customer service regarding sales and test drive bookings.

As a lead into this case study we suggest that you now undertake the activity on the next page which aims to help you to begin to develop an understanding of the problems encountered with the business operations of the Trusty Car Company. This will help you to begin to develop your own ideas, a list of questions and possibly associated assumptions regarding the case study that we will be working with.

The Trusty Car Company Group (TCCG) is a rapidly growing business. It was formed about two years ago by the merger of a number of garages who specialised in the sale of used cars. As the newly formed TCCG, the garages then became dealers for the Average Autos car manufacturer. Subsequently, as the business of each garage has expanded to cover the sale of new vehicles, the parts and servicing side of the business has also developed (as well as maintaining the sale of second-hand cars). The primary business of each garage is currently considered to be in car sales; each garage deals in both new and used cars. The used cars held at a particular garage come from a variety of sources; some from customer trade-ins at that garage, some from exchanges with other TCCG garages. Each garage aims to keep a limited number of second-hand cars in stock, depending on current trends within the group as well as local sales patterns. Cars are frequently moved between the five TCCG garages in the Trusty Car Group to avoid any car remaining on a forecourt for any great period (this activity is handled by the garage Manager).

In addition to used cars, each garage keeps a limited supply of new cars. These are available for customers to test drive or purchase. A record is maintained of all new cars on stock within the TCCG. If a customer requires a particular car (for test drive and/or purchase) and the local garage does not have the desired model or specification, the sales staff can check if another garage in the TCCG has one on stock. If one can be located then a transfer/exchange between garages is arranged by the Manager. If not, then, in the case of a purchase requirement, they can place an order with the Average Autos manufacturer. Although members of the sales staff can take bookings for test drives, the final authorisation rests with the Manager of the garage.

Each garage has a number of other departments; parts, servicing and administration. The primary purpose of the parts department is in supplying the service department and supporting car sales if any optional extras are required which are not factory fitted (e.g. sunroof, air conditioning, alloy wheels etc.). The parts department can also trade with customers directly. The service department at each garage has a variety of functions such as basic car servicing and valet service. A number handle MOTs. The small admin department takes care of staff administration functions (such as salaries, holiday and other leave of absence). The admin department may also handle booking in cars for the service department and general switchboard activities.

Figure 5.1: Trusty Car Company case study description

A: Take a few minutes to read through the Trusty Car Company case study description in figure 5.1. Try and pull out the key things that we might want to represent in a model of the company and its business. Keep in mind the preliminary analysis information described at the start of this section as this should be used to guide you. You will be able to compare your own ideas with those we present throughout this chapter. The following questions may give you something to focus on as you develop your thoughts and questions:

- What is the scope of the business that you are considering?
- Can you identify a system boundary?
- Be clear whether and when you are identifying the activities of a single member of the TCC group or the group as a whole. Which are you modelling, and does it matter?

Remember that the aim of the above activity is not that you develop a model at this stage. It just gives you the opportunity to examine the case study in more detail before you move on to review subsequent sections where we will begin to present a model of the TCC business and its associated problems.

5.2 Application of UML

The difficulty with tackling a problem like this is that we are presented with a lot of detail about the company and aspects of the business. Information overload. It is often difficult for us to clarify the real problem from all of this information – but this is exactly what we need to do. Developing a picture can help us enormously. The picture simplifies and clarifies the information that we have been given by identifying the *scope* of the problem. In modelling terms we talk about identifying the system boundary. This helps us to identify what is inside and outside our area of interest. This helps us, and our customer (in this case the company employees), clarify their thinking and provides us with a framework to develop ideas further.

We are going to begin developing the initial picture using UML use case notation. This will help us identify the scope of the problem by considering the requirements.

Through the following subsections we will develop a UML model for the TCC and its problems. The example solution is presented as a series of models developed incrementally throughout the chapter. This reflects the important characteristics of model development and methodologies discussed in Chapter 4, i.e. a key to success at each stage of the project is to develop *incrementally* and make use of planned *iterations* to review the progress of work. Each iteration considers an alternative level of information.

Q: *So how many iterations do you need? Is there a magic number? You might like to think about this as you read through the material contained in this chapter. We shall return to discuss this again later in the chapter.*

As a final point, remember that the models we develop through this chapter are not presented as exact solutions. The importance of telling you this is that if, in following our suggested activities, you develop an alternative model it does not necessarily mean that yours is wrong if it does not match ours (nor, of course, does it necessarily mean that ours is wrong either). Our example models are presented as one possible view to give you something to think about.

5.2.1 Use Case Model

In developing a use case model our main aim is to take the generally verbose (or sketchy) information we have about the problem and start to develop a picture that will help clarify and structure our thinking. We generally talk about this in supporting requirements capture. This will be done through a number of stages.

Initially, a number of key actors may come to mind, and perhaps a number of key requirements that will take the form of the use cases. Unless the problem is very simplistic it is infeasible to determine all key actors and requirements in one pass. The most realistic thing you should hope for is that this initial activity supports you in asking questions. At the outset of investigating an organisation's business problems you know you will have lots of questions to ask, but don't always know how to identify the questions in themselves. The approach we would advocate is to identify a few actors and use cases, draw the use case model and evaluate your findings. This instinctively suggests an iterative process. Never assume that you will determine all necessary information in a single pass.

In our own view, the initial actors that come to mind represent the **Customer** and the **Salesman**. There are a number of key activities that these roles are involved in, which were highlighted in the case study description and preliminary analysis. This information could begin to help us to determine a number of initial core use cases that these actors are engaged in. Note that there is an implication here that we chose to start by identifying the key actors and then determine use cases associated with those actors. This is a quite common way to start use case modelling i.e. drive the activity by identifying the actors of interest which help us to determine the system scope or boundary. Putting this information together, our initial use case diagram is suggested in figure 5.2.

At this point it is worth reflecting on the diagram in figure 5.2. Did you come up with additional actors and/or use cases? It is reasonable to make certain assumptions that might result in a very different model – these assumptions might concern roles and responsibilities of TCC employees or the scope of the business being considered. Assumptions are a natural part of the modelling process. They are necessary where you have to make reasoned guesses to fill in some immediate gaps in your knowledge. These assumptions need to be clarified at some point, and might typically form questions that you would want to clarify with appropriate project members. It is worth taking the time to write these assumptions down on paper. Avoid relying on your memory.

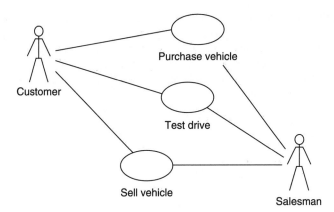

Figure 5.2 Initial use case diagram

In the case of the outline model in figure 5.2 we are making a clear statement concerning the initial scope of the problem. This initial scope focuses on the sale of vehicles and test drive bookings. This does not model the entire TCC business, but from the preliminary analysis introduced at the start of section 5.1 you might recall that we were not asked to do that. All we've started to do in figure 5.2 is outline a few key business requirements that we can work with further. This does not mean to say that your outline model is wrong if you took a broader view of the business – it might, in fact, help to see the elements we are focussing on in a broader context. The point is to be clear about your objective.

Before moving on, let us consider the importance of naming. The naming of use cases and actors is a tricky business, and can help or hinder the clarity of the model. The general guidance is that we want names to be as concise and yet as meaningful as possible. That is quite a tall order when you think about it. Considering the example diagram in figure 5.2, you might well be asking yourself what do we mean by the use case called **Test Drive**? Well, for clarity what we mean is the management of test drive bookings. That is the actual requirement, i.e. the thing that needs to be handled. It could be argued then that **Management of Test Drive Bookings** would be a better name. It certainly might, but it is a much longer name and gets in the way of the nice simple picture that we are trying to develop. Let's avoid getting overly tied up on the naming of a single use case and consider that the point we are making here is that it is important to think what you are trying to convey in the diagram. It is helpful to have names that are as short and as helpful as possible. In this initial model we are mostly concerned with highlighting that something needs to be considered within the scope of the modelling – and our diagram succeeds in getting test drives on the agenda. A further point concerns how self sufficient we expect a diagram to be, i.e. is it able to stand entirely on its own merits without any written or verbal explanation? Our own answer comes down to the fact that we want the diagram to add clarity to a situation under exploration – but that it does need more. Incidentally, before leaving this subject, consider what else could a use case called **Test Drive** have been about. The physical taking of the test drive is surely outside the system scope – isn't it?

We presented the use case diagram in figure 5.2 as an initial outline. It is not the whole picture. It merely starts to develop one aspect of the business requirements, and therefore helps us to identify the requirements that a potential computer system would need to support. The diagram in figure 5.3 identifies a further number of actors and an additional set of use cases. This time we are considering additional requirements that are not directly associated with the **Customer**.

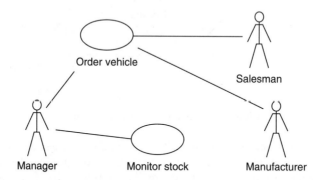

Figure 5.3: Additional actors and use cases

Q: *Considering the two diagrams presented so far in figures 5.2 and 5.3, you might notice that there is a lack of navigation shown. Is navigation helpful at this point? Consider how the addition of such additional notation might help – does it significantly alter the understanding at this point? If you need a reminder about navigation then you might like to refer back to Chapter 2. This question will be addressed in the text as you read on.*

The two use case diagrams shown in figure 5.2 and 5.3 can be combined to present a more complete picture. This is shown in figure 5.4. This raises an interesting point concerning modelling and the representation of models. There is a general desire on the part of many learning to use UML to put all the information into a single diagram in the belief that this is *correct*. The reality, as ever, is a little less clear cut than that and there may be many benefits to presenting the whole as a series of diagrams. It is important to stop thinking in terms of there being a single correct approach, and instead consider what is helpful. Think what you are trying to convey through one or more diagrams. Who is the information being presented to, and is there added clarity to be gained from breaking the diagram down or presenting it as a whole? Our recommendation is that you should avoid assuming that there is just the one correct approach to take.

An earlier question referred to a lack of navigation on the associations shown in use case diagrams in figures 5.2 and 5.3 (in fact all use case diagrams in this chapter). It is important to understand that a lack of shown navigation can generally mean one of two things. Either the association is bi-directional, or it is as yet unspecified. In the case of the model we are developing here we would clarify our use of the notation by saying that we have not yet decided on that level of detail (and in itself we don't think it entirely relevant at this stage). You might think that bi-directional should in fact have an arrow head on each side of the association. That would certainly make this explicit, and it is something we would encourage. However, you should be aware that not all UML drawing tools support such use of notation. For example, Rational Rose, which was used for the diagrams in this chapter, will not support showing bi-directional associations in such a way – they would in fact be shown by a lack of arrow head on either end of the association. This is just a further example of why the diagram itself may not include all necessary information, and additional clarification/explanation may be required in the form of accompanying documentation of annotations on the diagram at least.

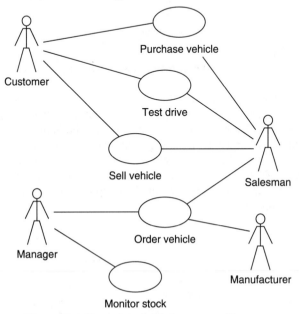

Figure 5.4 Complete initial use case diagram

The diagram in figure 5.4 represents one potential version of an initial use case diagram. This diagram aims to represent the business and system scope of relevance to the problem being investigated. At this point we need to revisit the case study description, review the preliminary analysis and ask ourselves if we think we have indeed captured an appropriate picture of the situation.

The initial activity in this chapter asked you to consider the representation of the individual garage from the group. In what ways is this distinction important? This again concerns the scope of the model. We shall consider this further as we explore a further possible refinement to the use case model, which is shown in figure 5.5. This latest refinement aims to capture the idea of the **TCC Group** through an actor. The use cases associated with this actor refer to group level activities concerning the location of vehicles and their exchange within the group. This is a rather fuzzy actor at the moment, and it is unclear whether this role refers to a person or a piece of software. In the longer term it may be unhelpful – but its sole purpose for now is to introduce the notion of the group into the picture and indicate the transfer of information and control between different garages in the group.

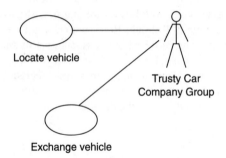

Figure 5.5 An additional actor and use cases

The additional information concerning the TCC Group and associated use cases can be added to the main diagram. Consider for a moment that there might be additional elaborations to the mode that we could make at this point. Perhaps there are other use cases that we can identify that our actors are engaged in? Although these might not all be within our eventual system scope, they might help us to increase our understanding of the roles played by our actors. This in itself helps us to develop a clearer understanding of the overall business. Consider the diagram in figure 5.6. This represents our suggestion for a second version of our developing use case diagram.

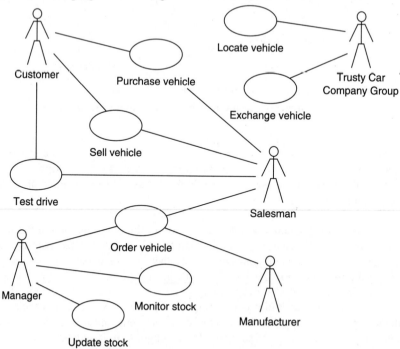

Figure 5.6 Second version of use case diagram

The second version use case diagram includes the additional information shown in figure 5.5, but also takes a broader view of the use cases that the **Manager** actor is engaged with. All we know about the **Manager** from previous use case diagrams (figure 5.4) is that the actor is involved in **Order Vehicle** and **Monitor Stock** use cases. The additional use case, **Update Stock**, shown in figure 5.6, makes clearer that the **Manager** is also responsible for the updating of stock information. Updating stock information may take into account the movement of stock within the group, as well as the result of selling and purchasing vehicles (these are all assumptions that we would have to clarify).

In the second complete version of the use case diagram we have clearly expanded the scope of the system being modelled. At this point let us consider an alternative incremental development of the use case diagram, which concerns elaborating the detail presented in the use cases, while maintaining the current scope. This leads to our next, and final, revision being shown in the use case diagram in figure 5.7.

The expansion we have examined concerns use cases involving the **Customer** and **Salesman** actors only, and for this reason figure 5.7 only represents this sub-diagram. The diagram explores an extra level of detail; namely the requirement to **Price Deal**, and importantly the point being made that this requirement is common to both **Sell Vehicle** and **Purchase Vehicle** use cases.

This is a good example which helps us to see when a sub-diagram is relevant. In this case, we would argue that expanding the level of information presented in the overall use case diagram just clutters the view. The main use case diagram is most helpful when it presents a clear scope of the problem, in terms of all actors and key use cases of the same level of detail. By *same level* we mean higher level use cases and use cases that are evidently moving down to make design or implementation decisions. There is little to be gained by adding more and more information to the single diagram, in particular where the result is that you have a mixture of use cases at different levels – in fact it tends to just become confusing. Having said all of that of course, it is not necessarily wrong to include such information to a single use case diagram if there is a reason to do so.

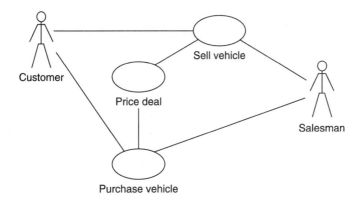

Figure 5.7: Use case sub-diagram

Q: *At this point you might like to consider other elements of the business that our model does not represent. For example, there is no concept of accounting and money transfer. Is this an oversight, or is it outside the scope of the model? This is something that we will return to discuss later in this chapter.*

The introduction to this case study talked about developing a model of the business and its requirements. You may have observed though that we have not chosen to use any of the particular UML business modelling notation associated with use case modelling.

A: Consider redrawing one or more of the use case diagrams in this section using the business modelling variants of use case modelling notation (refer to Appendix A for details of the notation if you are unfamiliar with this). Consider what is to be gained by using thse business modelling variants of the use case diagram – or more specifically, what is lost? Solutions to this activity can be found on the Web site which accompanies this book (details of which were given in the preface).

5.2.2 Class Model

The requirements capture exercise in the previous section has helped us to develop a clearer picture of the problems experienced by the business. These are candidate areas that require attention by the refinement of business processes and/or support through technology by developing an information system of sorts. In this section we are going to consider the development of a class diagram. The class diagram helps us to begin to identify the static structure that would support the requirements that we identified through the use case diagram activity. The point being there is a clear link to be made between the use case and class diagrams.

LINK POINT	Class diagram provides static structure that should support requirements identified through use case diagram.

At this point you might want to refer back to Chapter 2, where we identified a number of guidelines for identifying classes and objects and rules for refining the candidate list. Keep in mind though that these are only guidelines. There are no automated or guaranteed process that will identify the classes for you it is a matter of using a number of techniques to test out your class design. This is a point we will return to later.

A: Look again at the case study description introduced at the start of this chapter in figure 5.1. Determine a number of candidate classes for the Trusty Car Company and refine them by applying the rules for rejecting objects and classes that were covered in Chapter 2. A solution to this activity will be presented as this case study develops (so try and do the activity without looking too far ahead).

Our recommendation is that you start with a simple number of intuitive classes and identify associations between them. Again, assume that you are going to develop the model incrementally through a number of iterations. Allow the model to develop through these iterations. Develop something simple to begin with, and then enter into a model review process.

We hope to demonstrate such a review process through the following series of class diagrams that we will present in this section. A number of versions is presented, with each considering an alternative level of information. Remember that with each step of model development the model does not necessarily become larger. An initial diagram is shown in figure 5.8. This initial model merely shows a number of named candidate classes. Our point in showing this relates directly to the process – you should not wait until you have all the necessary information before you start trying to draw the diagram – the act of drawing the diagram is part of the process and can help focus your mind.

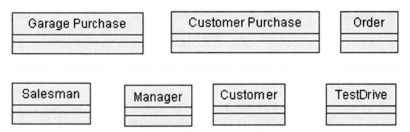

Figure 5.8: First iteration – initial set of classes

We immediately test out these classes by attempting to form associations between them. This refined diagram is shown in figure 5.9. This immediately helps you to reconcile the classes you have identified – if you cannot draw associations then perhaps you have a class that is not within the appropriate system scope, or perhaps it is an attribute of another class?

In considering the TCC case study, a particular issue is the representation of the actual cars in the system. How might you approach this? In thinking ahead you might consider that this might be implemented as a database, which the developing system needs to interface to. We choose to avoid making such implementation decisions at this stage and assume there will be a Vehicles class, which represents a set of all vehicles. This is mostly a reminder that class diagrams do not need to be down at the software level. Indeed, in terms of clarifying communication between participants in a project they are most helpful when kept above that level.

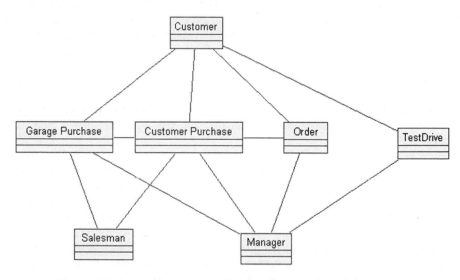

Figure 5.9: Second iteration – initial classes with associations

The third version of the class diagram, including the **Vehicles** class and relevant associations is shown in figure 5.10. Note that as with the use case diagram we have chosen not to add navigation information at this stage. This is a conscious decision on our part not to over elaborate the model at this time.

 A: Consider the **Vehicles** class in figure 5.10 and the explanation of what it represents. What alternative approaches might you consider? What are the strengths and weaknesses of each approach? Do any of them add further clarity? Solutions to this activity can be found on the Web site which accompanies this book (details of which were given in the preface).

Look closely at the class diagram in figure 5.10 and consider its merits as a developing object oriented design. You might recall from your previous OO studies, that two characterisations of a design concern the level of *coupling* and *cohesion*.

Coupling concerns the number of connections/associations between classes. This gives a measure of the dependency between classes in the system, and it is argued that a low level of coupling is desirable in good OO design i.e. the fewer associations the better. Looking at the diagram in 5.10 you might argue there is a high level of coupling, i.e. lots of associations between lots of classes. Are these all appropriate? Well, in developing the design further it is important to test out the validity of associations.

 Q: *What techniques do you know about that might help you to test the validity of associations in a class diagram? This is something that we will return to discuss later in this chapter.*

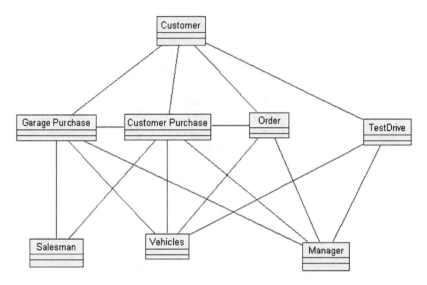

Figure 5.10: Third iteration – addition of Vehicles class

Cohesion concerns the level of detail represented in each class, and concerns the granularity of the design. Through exploring the cohesion of a class diagram we might consider that some classes are too high level (and therefore we need to split a single class into one or more separate classes) or too low level (in which case the classes may become attributes of other existing classes). Another outcome might be that we identify redundancy in the diagram, in particular the potential to introduce inheritance to help refactor the model. In considering the cohesion of the model shown in figure 5.10, we might consider a series of further refinements.

You may consider additional ones, but the following are the key refinements that we would like to suggest we consider introducing at this point:

- **Customer Purchase** and **Garage Purchase** are now regarded as specialisations of **Transaction** (figure 5.11).

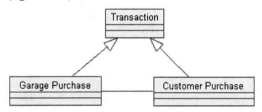

Figure 5.11: The generalisation, *Transaction*

- **Manager** and **Salesman** are specialisations of a generalised **Employee** class (figure 5.12).

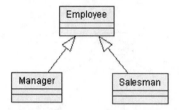

Figure 5.12: The generalisation, *Employee*

In addition a **Garage** class has been added to represent each physical member of the group. Finally, **Order** is composed of individual **OrderLine** (figure 5.13).

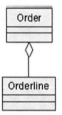

Figure 5.13: Identification of individual order lines

The above modifications have been incorporated into a fourth iteration of the class diagram, shown in figure 5.14.

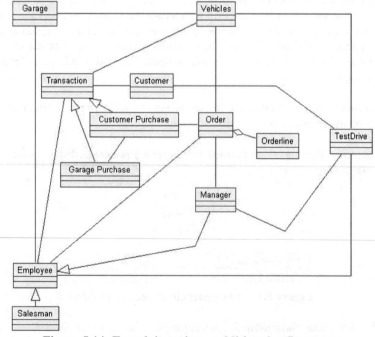

Figure 5.14: Fourth iteration – additional refinements

What more is there to consider at this point? Are we satisfied with the scope of the system being considered? Thinking back to the case study description in figure 5.1, we might at this point consider again the boundaries of the system that we have now described in the class diagram in figure 5.14. It might be appropriate to consider the need to interface with other systems. We already know about other departments within the TCC organisation, and our current model does not appear to reflect much beyond the recording of sales transactions. It might be appropriate to consider interfacing to other systems, for example, interfacing with a system in the Accounts department, or the option to perform a credit check on a customer before proceeding with a sales transaction.

An earlier question in section 5.2.1 asked you to think about the scope of the system again and how interfacing to such external systems or business units might be shown. We could have chosen to show these external systems as actors and associate them with appropriate use cases associated with the purchase of vehicles. It may be that we did not consider such matters until we got to this point in the class modelling exercise – and it may be appropriate to return to modify the use case diagram at this point. There is a similar argument that says as long as we have this information captured somewhere in the overall model of our problem (in this case the class diagram) then it does not matter about that level of detail being omitted on the use case diagram.

A: At this point return to modify the use case diagram in figure 5.6 (or your own diagrams if you have been drawing your own solutions) and add the additional information to illustrate interfacing to external systems as described above. Solutions to this activity can be found on the Web site which accompanies this book.

Consider the proposal in the sub-diagram diagram in figure 5.15 where we have introduced two interfaces.

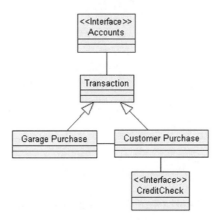

Figure 5.15: Interfaces to other systems

The interface called **Accounts** is shown as a place holder to show a possible link into an external accounts system. The second interface, called **CreditCheck**, is shown to represent a possible link point to a system to perform credit checks on customers before committing to a sales transaction. These are again points that we would want to clarify with the customer – but they appear sensible options to consider. When developing an IT system it is desirable to look at additional business benefits of exchanging information between complimentary systems, for example, as in this case to identify potential link points to other systems.

This additional interface information is incorporated in the fifth and final iteration of the class diagram in figure 5.15. Notice that that class diagram becomes larger as we progress through each iteration. This is one consequence of the iterative development. You might well expect that the model becomes larger with each progressive step. We would argue though that larger is not necessarily better, and you might well find that a subsequent iteration moves to a simpler model by excluding or combining classes from a previous iteration. With each model review we should be asking questions about the current scope and level of the model – and review what we consider to be appropriate for our present objectives.

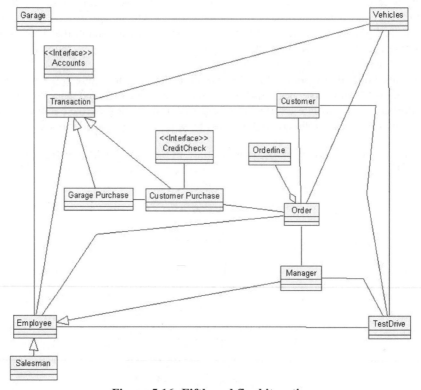

Figure 5.16: Fifth and final iteration

Let's return now to consider our current, and increasingly complex, class diagram. You will have noticed that as a result of the increasing size of the diagram, the layout has become more cluttered and generally awkward.

The point about layout is not entirely about the aesthetic qualities of the diagrams. The layout can affect our understanding of a diagram. This might be helpful in directing our attention to one or more key associations, or it might be unhelpful by implying a significance that does not exist. For example, in figure 5.16 there are four classes (**Employee**, **Garage**, **Vehicles** and **TestDrive**) that clearly mark the rectangular outline of the diagram. These appear to present a sort of boundary to the diagram. In actual fact this is just coincidental and no extra meaning is to be inferred. At times though the layout, in particular groupings of model components, may assist us in presenting additional information. The point is that we need to be aware of the possible hidden implications of the layout and avoid them when necessary.

A: Can you find a better way to lay this diagram out? Consider this either as a manual paper and pencil exercise, or lay it out in a tool of your choice. Many modelling tools (such as Rational Rose) provide a function to adjust the layout of diagram automatically. You may like to experiment with such a utility and see the result (you might gather that it is not often desirable). Alternative examples can be found on the Web site which accompanies this book.

Sometimes it is unavoidable that the resulting model presents a complex picture when viewed as a single diagram. At times the single diagram may be appropriate, but note that it is acceptable to work with partial views, as we did in figures 5.10, 5.11, 5.12 and 5.15. It is not necessary to take account of all of the information at all times in a single diagram.

5.2.3 Interaction Diagram

Interaction diagrams provide a vehicle to express the modelling of message passing between objects. In order to consider objects, we need to have some understanding of the classes involved. In order to be able to move on to modelling dynamic behaviours we need an agreement on a set of classes. This does not mean that all class modelling activities need to be complete, such that we have a final class diagram, before considering interactions. In fact a key benefit of interaction diagrams is that they allow us to test out our developing class diagram to see if we have an appropriate structure to represent the requirements. This exercise can help us to determine if a set of classes do take part in a scenario as we anticipate. This helps us to assess whether classes are redundant or missing from our overall model of the system – or whether appropriate associations have been identified.

LINK POINT	The Interaction diagram (either sequence diagram or collaboration diagram) help to test that the static model represented in the **class diagram** will support the requirements identified in the **use case diagram**

Remember that interaction diagrams have many applications. One key application concerns the documenting of individual use cases by tracing scenarios within them. We are going to look at a number of scenarios with regard to this case study. Consider the Trusty Car

Company use case diagrams developed earlier in this chapter. For example, look back and consider figure 5.6. Specifically, consider the **Test Drive** use case and the possible scenarios that it might involve – involving both successful and unsuccessful outcomes. Consider the following activity to help you think about this further.

A: Take a few moments to put together an interaction diagram (your choice – either sequence or collaboration) showing one such scenario related to the **Test Drive** use case. At this point you will need to refer to the class diagram to identify which objects will interact in satisfying the use case scenario. When you have an outline of your own interaction diagrams (or when you are completely stuck!) refer to the example solutions that we will present as you work through this chapter and consider some of the questions raised.

The following example solution is presented as a series of models. Each interaction diagram that we will present considers an alternative scenario. The first version, shown in figure 5.17, considers the scenario showing a successful booking of test drive, with the vehicle located at the same garage where the booking takes place.

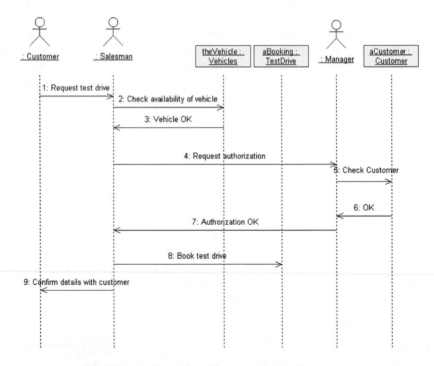

Figure 5.17: Scenario showing successful test drive booking

Q: *Is it more helpful, appropriate or correct to show interactions between objects of* **Customer** *and* **Salesman** *or instances of the* **Customer** *and* **Salesman** *actors? This question will be addressed in the text as you read on.*

When we are using the interaction diagram to document one or more use cases it is often helpful to include initial interactions between instances of actors. It is these initial interactions that influence and subsequently trigger the internal behaviour of the use case. This in turn allows us to check if we have identified appropriate actors and explored their association with use cases. Too often we become distracted by the internal workings of the business or system that we are considering and forget to give adequate attention to the triggers.

In considering this it is important that you remember the distinction between an instance of an actor and the internal manifestation of the actor as an object in the system (remember the avatar discussion from Chapter 2 – if not you might like to go back and read that now). The question earlier on this page was really to see if you were comfortable with the distinction between an actor (such as **Customer** and **Salesman**) and an instance of a **Customer** object. Remember back in Chapter 2 we talked about the distinction between an actor that may represent a role played by a person or thing outside of the system, and the internal representation of the person or thing. The latter is often referred to as an avatar. In considering interactions it is important, as in this case to make a distinction between interactions that involve an instance of the **Customer** actor and an instance of the **Customer** class.

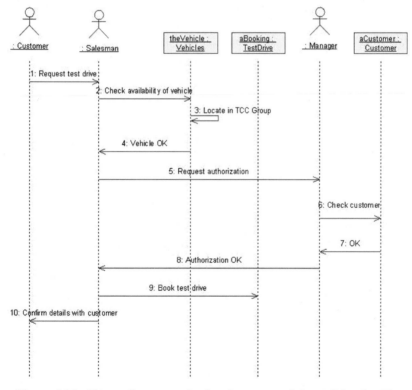

Figure 5.18: Alternative scenario showing successful test drive booking

Each scenario represents a possible path through the use case. So, while the scenario in figure 5.17 may be a logical place to start there are other scenarios that we might consider. For example, figure 5.18 shows such an alternative scenario representing a situation where the vehicle is *not* found locally and has to be located elsewhere within the group. The overall outcome of the scenario remains successful as the test drive is booked at its completion.

Q: *The scenario presented in figure 5.18 brings out something quite specific about the business operation. What are the implications of the **Manager** being involved in this scenario? Does the **Manager** have to be involved in this or is it something the **Salesman** can do? This is something we will address in the subsequent section when we consider activity diagrams.*

A third example scenario is shown in figure 5.19. This suggests a scenario where the outcome is not successful as it considers a situation where the **Manager** decides to decline the test drive. It is unclear *why* or under what circumstances the **Manager** does this. In order to explore this further we would need to have a better understanding of the company's operational procedures. For example, is the decision based on some check made against the **Customer**? If so, then we should maybe try and capture that in the model. Are we correct in thinking that the **Manager** deals with the customer directly in this situation?

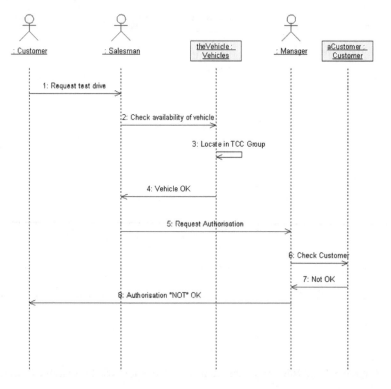

Figure 5.19: Scenario showing unsuccessful test drive booking

A: At this point take a few moments to write out an English language description of the use case **Test Drive**. In doing so you might consider other scenarios that were not covered by the sequence diagrams presented in this section. Solutions to this activity can be found on the Web site which accompanies this book.

Hopefully this section has provided some answers to a question posed back in section 5.2.2 concerning techniques to help you to test out your developing class model – in particular the appropriateness of associations between classes. The CRC card technique can also help you in this area. These were discussed more fully in Chapter 2.

LINK POINT	The **Class Responsibility Collaboration (CRC)** card technique can also help to test the developing class diagram and its ability to support a range of use cases. The CRC technique could help to develop and clarify the interaction diagram, by carrying out a walkthrough of the object interactions. Although not part of UML it is a helpful technique to remember about. There was an information box on this subject in the case study in Chapter 2. If you have not come across CRC cards before, or you would generally like to read more on this subject, then you might like to follow some of our recommended readings on this topic at the end of Chapter 2.

Q: *We have no indication of how long this vehicle location and transfer may take i.e. to move a vehicle within the group ... is this important? If it were important, how might we annotate the sequence diagram to show this information? This question will be addressed in the text as you read on.*

In this section we have presented a total of three sequence diagrams. You might well be wondering how many of these diagrams are appropriate in any situation. Our view is that the interaction diagram is best used to highlight one or more key scenarios – in particular where there is a key issue that needs to be clarified amongst a project team. Beyond experimenting with the notation itself, it is rarely necessary to draw out an interaction diagram for every conceivable scenario. Other techniques may provide sufficient description to identify key issues. For example, the documentation of a use case by using English language, or using an activity diagram where it is much easier to incorporate alternative behaviours and outcomes. If you carried out the activity earlier in this section concerning the writing out of an English language description of the *Test Drive Booking* use case you might have clearly identified the key inputs, outputs and exceptional behaviour sufficiently. The interaction diagram may be used to highlight one or more of the key scenarios, especially where clarification is being sought with other project members.

Note that in this section we have shown a preference for using sequence diagrams as opposed to collaboration diagrams. We find the sequence diagrams more visually appealing, and naturally more easy to follow. There are good reasons for using each of these types of diagrams in different situations. You might have an alternative view, or certainly a different preference, though it is important to remember that both options exist.

A: At this point we suggest that you might find it helpful to experiment with collaboration diagrams. Take one (or more) of the sequence diagrams from figures in this section and redraw it as a collaboration diagram (solutions are provided on the Web site which accompanies this book). You can either do this as a pencil and paper exercise, or use the modelling tool of your choice. Many modelling tools (such as Rational Rose) support automatic conversion between the two types of interaction diagram. Do you consider it more helpful to use one or other of the interaction diagrams in this situation? Do you have a natural tendancy to want to use one or other of the interaction diagrams?

5.2.4 Activity Diagrams

The previous section looked at examples of modelling interactions between objects. In particular, to document scenarios within individual use cases. There are times when we want to consider a broader picture, for example to consider alternative outcomes – especially where we consider there is potential for a bottleneck to occur. While it is true to say that UML notation supports alternative outcomes being shown on a single interaction diagram they become overly complex when you try to do so. This is also something that many modelling tools do not support well. Fortunately, UML provides us with a much easier way of documenting alternative behaviours and outcomes, and this will be explored further in this section concerning activity diagrams.

LINK POINT	The **activity diagram** can help to highlight alternative behaviours. This can help to elaborate on the documentation of **use cases**, in particular raising dependencies that may lead to bottlenecks in business or system processes.

A: Consider the information that you have acquired through the previous sections in this chapter concerning the Trusty Car Company case study. In particular the interaction diagrams related to the test drive booking and the use case model. We are going to explore this further in this section, but spend five minutes now to identify and understand possible dependencies that can affect the booking of a test drive. Think about the process of authorising the test drive booking. What is required?

There are a number of dependencies that you might identify. The one we are going to focus on here concerns the fact that a **Manager** needs to be involved in the process of booking the test drive. It is therefore important that the **Manager** is available. The successful booking of a test drive depends on this.

A: Develop an activity diagram that shows the dependency concerning the availability of the **Manager** in authorising a test drive booking. When you have an outline of your own activity diagram (or when you are completely stuck!) have a look at the example solution presented in this chapter as you read on.

An initial solution which begins to show the dependency on the **Manager** is shown in the activity diagram shown in figure 5.20. This diagram shows a swimlane for each of the key participants (if you cannot remember about swimlanes you might like to look at the notation refresher in Chapter 2 or Appendix A). The **Customer** is the actor who initiates the use case, the **Salesman** is the actor who initially interacts with the **Customer**, and the **Manager** is the actor who carries out the authorisation. In figure 5.20 we have used the swimlane notation to make a clear division between the activities being carried out by the participants. We've also used a combination of activities and states in these swimlanes to try and capture key points (and as a reminder that you can do that on activity diagrams).

A: Before carrying on with this section, take 10 minutes and consider the activity diagram in figure 5.20 (or your own if you have prepared an alternative based on the previous activity in this section). Take a sheet of paper and write down a list of questions that the diagram makes you ask. These might be questions concerning the diagram and what it is intending to show, or it might be concerning omissions regarding the business knowledge. Hopefully, some of the questions that you raise will be considered in the remainder of this section – we will also be raising a few more questions of our own to make you think.

A number of questions are raised by the activity diagram in figure 5.20. Remember that each modelling activity you undertake and each diagram that you draw will possibly raise as many questions as it answers. This should not necessarily be seen as a bad thing. The aim is to get into a position where you are asking the right questions. We'll look further at some of the questions the diagram makes us ask as we continue through this section.

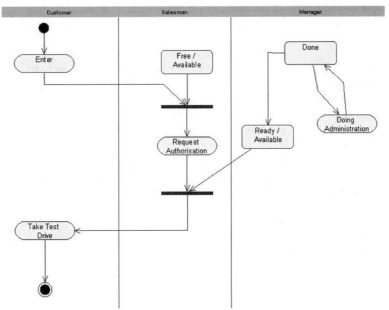

Figure 5.20: Activity diagram showing dependencies

Let's consider the importance of naming again, and what makes an appropriate or helpful activity. Looking at the figure 5.20, the **Customer** is shown to have an activity called **Take Test Drive**. Is this likely, or even a possible outcome of this use case? This is perhaps a matter of scope. If we consider the view that the use case is considered to represent a requirement of the system to support the business, then it will not, in itself, be associated with physically taking a vehicle out on a test drive. Unless, perhaps, we assume that each of the garages vehicles are relaying telemetry back to the system? This is stretching things a little, but hopefully you see the point we are making. That does not necessarily make the **Take Test Drive** activity invalid in the diagram in figure 5.20 – the diagram is about clarity and all such diagrams should help to move you to a better point of understanding the problem. In each situation consider what is in and out of scope, and what the diagram is aiming to achieve.

Something that was missing from the interaction diagrams in the previous section is what happens if there is no car found locally at the particular garage? How do we show the **Manager** arranging a group transfer? What if there is no vehicle within the group? Do we then check stock orders to see if a group member will be receiving the required specification vehicle in the near future? Do we just substitute a close match vehicle for the customer? Who informs the customer? Okay, we don't have the information here to answer all of these questions, but we can modify our activity diagram to raise this issue, and this may then serve as a useful diagram for the project team to discuss.

There are questions concerning clarification of roles and responsibilities amongst actors, and these concern the TCC business procedures. For example, is it always the **Salesman** who gets back to the **Customer**? What happens if the **Manager** decides not to authorise the test drive due to bad customer reference or for some other reason? Let's now consider two alternative activity diagrams. The diagrams in figure 5.21 show a different approach to the **Test Drive Booking** activity.

These alternative diagrams take into account one of the questions raised from our review of the first diagram, namely the need to locate a suitable vehicle. That was something that our original diagram in figure 5.20 did not consider. The diagrams in figure 5.21 show alternative outcomes, i.e. the test drive booking being authorised or not, thus giving a much broader description of the outcomes of the **Test Drive Booking** use case.

Examine the activity diagrams in figure 5.21 carefully. Which is a more suitable representation of the actual activity; the sequential representation in figure 5.21a, or figure 5.21b which shows the salesman having two parallel threads of activities?

 Q: *At the stage of the **Manager** carrying out the **Arrange Transfer** activity, what happens if a match is not found within the group? Do we go back to the customer with alternative suggestions? Do we check stock orders to see if a group member will be receiving the required specification vehicle in the near future? Do we just substitute a close match vehicle for the customer?*

The answer to the above question could lead us to an alternative activity diagram as that could be considered a different scenario. Alternatively, a further series of activities could be added to the diagrams in figure 5.21 to raise this issue more explicitly. In any event, it raises questions that are best resolved by further discussion with TCC employees (and takes us beyond the scope of the case study here).

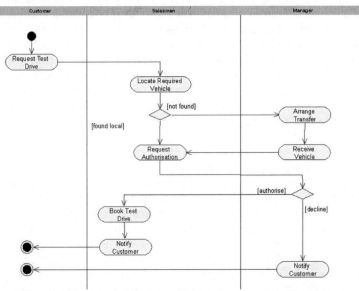

Figure 5.21a: Activity diagram showing test drive booking

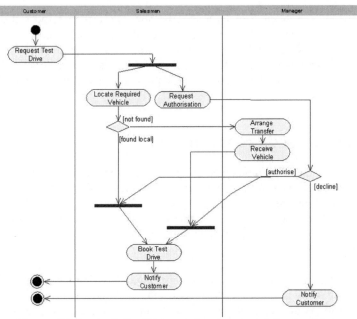

Figure 5.21b: Activity diagram showing test drive booking

Q: *What considerations/impact is there of the implied time delay between the **Manager** activities of **Arrange Transfer** and **Receive Vehicle**?*

When you come to think about it there are broader implications of timing and availability other than the one mentioned in the above question. What considerations/impact is there of the implied time delay between the **Manager** activities? How long may it take the **Manager** to become available? We've been really very general, and perhaps too vague in identifying the task associating the **Manager** with **Doing Accounts** (from figure 5.20 that was the only activity we associated with the **Manager** that could make him unavailable). What other activities is this actor involved in that might block him? What happens in the event of holiday or sick leave? If it is possible that this whole activity could "block" then this is surely a problem from the point of view of the business as well as any system to be implemented.

The issue remains concerning what happens to the customer during all this? The activity diagram seems to show that the customer is suspended while the booking process is followed through. Does this matter? Well, we might argue that we're being a bit pernickety if we try and represent that in the activity diagrams in this section, but it does raise an interesting point about the timing again and how long the customer might be left hanging around. Each of the three activity diagrams we've shown certainly end with the customer, since the end state is located in the **Customer** swimlane. The **Manager** and **Salesman** end with a **Notify Customer** activity. What is the difference between these? One is certainly a positive outcome, the other negative as far as the customer is concerned (reflected in the different termination states in the **Customer** swimlane). Is this a realistic representation?

The end states on the diagram in figure 5.21b show two different end states. This is an attempt to make it clear that the end states reached have a different meaning. Is that a helpful thing to try and show? To answer that we would need to consider the benefits to be gained by showing alternative end states. Perhaps it depends on whether this diagram feeds into another, which would show further consequences of the different end states having been reached.

5.3 Summary and discussion

This initial case study has contained a great many questions and activities. That is deliberate, because we wanted to ensure that you had plenty of opportunities to engage with the material and think things through for yourself. No doubt each of the questions and activities had you also asking yourself further questions. Don't be put off by this. Coming up with the questions is a key part of the modelling activity, and often one of the most difficult.

A key point of this case study has been to think about clarifying the purpose of the model. Specifically addressing the scope of the model, and ideally not taking on more in the model than you need to. With each problem you tackle there is a temptation to broaden out the model, such that you end up trying to model the Universe if you are not careful. Whilst this can be interesting in itself, it rarely helps you understand the problem at hand and just confuses any customer and your fellow modellers.

Looking back at the case study, we've tried to emphasise the link points between the various UML diagram types. As each is introduced it gives us further clarification about a part of the business and its operations. This reaffirms that a single diagram at a single level will rarely be sufficient – any business model you develop will likely be composed of a number of different UML diagrams, and within each diagram type a number of iterations/revisions or sub-diagrams providing additional detail.

This case study described a problem with many typical characteristics of problems faced by business and systems analysts on a daily basis. The complexities involved with coming to grips with an organisation's business and being able to determine clearly what the problem is from the general noise.

As a final summary of points from this case study, the following are our recommended guidelines for applying UML to a modelling exercise similar to that presented in this case study:

Focus	Strive for continued focus on defining the problem – what is the problem that we are trying to address?
Ever decreasing circles	Iterations are good, and a necessary means to work through problems. But know when to cut off. Avoid falling into the trap of thinking that more and more detail is necessarily better or more correct.
Less may indeed be more	Consider that an iteration may actually result in a less complex diagram i.e. less information being presented as you refine and adjust the scope of the problem or level of detail being considered.
Questions are good	Okay, we need to ensure that we get some answers along the way too, but if each diagram you draw raises questions then it is working and it is a good diagram. Be very afraid if people just look at the first diagram that you draw and say its "okay". It probably means that they either don't understand (is your diagram too complex?) or are not taking the necessary time to think through the implications and ideas presented in the model.
Dialogue, dialogue and more dialogue	People have got to keep communicating, checking progress and correcting the direction of the project as appropriate. This dialogue is best supported by the questions raised through the development of the model.
Choices	If you are wanting to highlight or explore alternative behaviours in a system then we recommend using the activity diagram as opposed to an interaction diagram.
Think broad	Look at applying a wide range of modelling techniques to help build up an incremental picture. Use UML diagrams to cross check other model views and reaffirm the problem to be solved.

Further reading

There aren't any specific readings that we would like to associate with this case study. If there are points concerning the use of notation that you are unfamiliar with at this stage we would recommend that you revisit Chapter 2. Hopefully that chapter, and its associated further readings will help to address some, if not all, of your queries.

6

Playing Games

The focus for this case study will be on designing computer-based games. This will include important issues in the use of class diagrams, discussion of the benefits of states and interaction diagrams. There are issues concerning Internet-based systems that benefit from examination of UML facilities for describing deployment. In particular, this case study will examine mechanisms for exploiting abstraction and for describing implementation. These points are summarised in the following *UML Used in this Chapter* information box.

UML Used in this Chapter	**USE CASE DIAGRAM**	to examine and capture requirements of the business and therefore of some system that may potentially support the business.
	STATECHART	to illustrate the internal behaviour of objects.
	CLASS DIAGRAM	to examine system structure.
	INTERACTION DIAGRAM	to express system dynamics.
	DEPLOYMENT DIAGRAM	to examine implementation issues.

We begin with development of a simple two-player game in a single computer environment. Examples of this sort are common in books on object-oriented design, including those specifically on UML. Indeed one of the authors co-authored an earlier textbook on UML where such examples were used. We leave it to the reader to determine whether the exposition which follows adds to these.

6.1 Case study introduction

We already know that this case study is going to be about designing games, specifically multi player games. The initial focus concerns the design and development of a simple two player game program, called *Battleships and Cruisers*. How can we model this? Well, begin by looking at the problem statement described in figure 6.1, which provides an outline description of the problem and requirements of the game.

Battleships and Cruisers is a two-player game. It uses two equal sized grids of squares, representing each player's view of an area of sea. A square starts off blank but can be marked by the player to whom it belongs with a battleship, a submarine or a cruiser token. Each player has the same number of battleship, cruiser and submarine tokens.

There are two phases in the game.

First, each player places each of their tokens on one of the empty squares on their grid, as shown below. Each token may be placed anywhere on the grid, so long as each square has at most one token. A player is not allowed to see where their opponent's tokens are placed.

Second, each player in turn tries to guess where their opponent's tokens are. After each guess the rules are consulted to decide if any points have been scored. If the square chosen has a battleship, three points are scored, if a submarine, 2 points, and if a cruiser, one point. Once a player has discovered all their opponent's tokens or after a fixed number of turns, the game is complete.

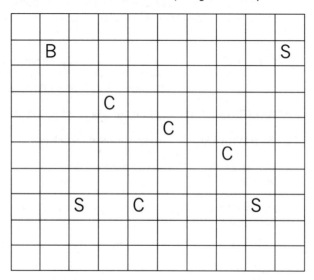

Example of Battleships and Cruisers   **Grid**

Figure 6.1: *Battleships and Cruisers* problem statement

A: Take a few minutes to read through the above problem statement figure 6.1. Try and pull out the key things that we might want to represent in a model of the game as presented. Think about intial use cases and actors, as well as possible candidate objects and classes. You will be able to compare your own ideas with those we present throughout this chapter.

6.2 Application of UML

Through the following sections we will develop a range of models using UML that help us to explore and further understand issues arising from this case study. As in the previous chapter, we will begin by looking at a simple use case model to help clarify the focus of the case study before proceeding into further details.

6.2.1 Use Case Model

The basic use case model is very simple. We will not look to complicate it here and so we find that figure 6.2 with a single type of actor and a single use case is perfectly adequate. If we wanted we could add an actor for the **Umpire**.

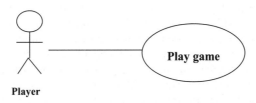

Player

Figure 6.2: Simplest use case diagram for a board game.

Q: *Alternatively we may find that we wish to distinguish two forms of player, where one is a human and the other a computer program. What criteria might be used to decide if this was necessary? What additional features of use case diagrams might be useful?*

6.2.2 Class Model

We identify objects in our problem statement in the usual way, by looking for nouns and noun phrases (we described this process more fully in Chapter 2 and you might find it helpful to refer back to that at this point). Each of these can be underlined and becomes a candidate for an object in our solution. We can eliminate some objects by some simple rules. We must make sure that our objects fit in with our use cases. In following through this process we would suggest that one possible set of classes we could be left with are the following:

- X player
- Y player
- Grid
- Rules

For reasons of ease of description we will call the object that contains the rule and score checking for the game the **Umpire**. When we make this sort of naming decision, we should really keep a note of the old name or names that this one replaces, just as we should record our decisions to select one synonym, when that rule for elimination is applied.

As we saw in the bank case study in Chapter 2, there is a general question about whether we need to have objects within a system to represent external actors (you might want to refer back to the discussion on these avatars in Chapter 2 at this point). There are no general answers; the best way is to proceed with such objects included and to look very hard at whether or not they bring any benefits to the solution. In the bank case study the avatar object was needed, since the system had to remember the details of each customer's accounts and maintain a permanent link from the actor to this information, even when the actor ceased interacting with the system. The **Customer** object provided a persistent record of the bank's view of the customer.

In this case, we have a **Player** actor in the use case model and we also include objects representing the players within the program. If the **Player** is to be computer controlled, this need is obvious. However, it is often useful to model any highly interactive association between an actor and the system with an internal object for that actor, to decouple the internal logic from the mechanism for human computer interaction. Players are free to decide on their moves in different ways, without us having to change the behaviour of the Grids, on one hand, or the way in which any human player interacts with the system, on the other.

To meet the desire for low coupling, we would prefer the associations shown in the initial class diagram, figure 6.3a, to link the two **PlayerObjects** and the **Grid**, with one way navigability. If this was only from **PlayerObject** to **Grid**, it would allow PlayerObjects to be reused without **Grid** forming part of the new solution. For reasons that will become obvious soon, **Player** and **Umpire** must be closely coupled with **Grid**, however. Although this prevents simple reuse, it gives us a strong indication that what we have may be a *pattern*.

Instead of decoupling **Player** by limiting the navigability of its associations, we use a generalisation, **PlayerObject**, to model its interaction with **Grid**. This generalisation is coupled, but its specialisations are still to be defined. Thus, the specific logic of the two types of player does not affect their behaviour when communicating with the **Grid**. This leads to the revised class diagram in figure 6.3b.

Umpire needs to know about **Grid** and each **PlayerObject** must know about **Grid**. Either each **PlayerObject** must know about **Umpire**, coupling everything, or the **Grid** must know about the Umpire and act as the communication mechanism between them. The latter solution couples **Umpire** tightly with **Grid**, which is again not apparently desirable. However, we can also make **Umpire** a generalisation, defining only the interaction with **Grid**. Such abstraction of common behaviour from specific behaviour is actually a very powerful concept. We will return to this issue later.

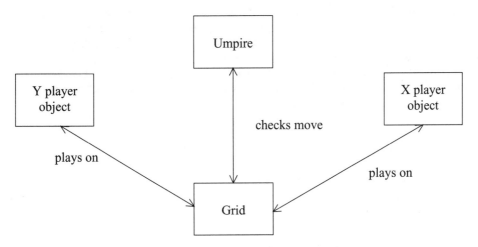

Figure 6.3a: Initial class diagram for a game

Each **PlayerObject** has one **Grid**. Only one **Umpire** exists, but it must deal with two grids. This set of relationships only applies in terms of communication among the objects defined.

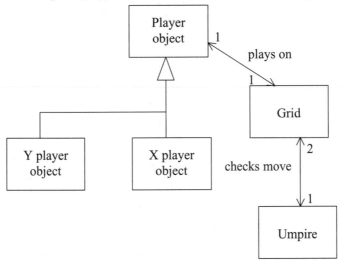

Figure 6.3b: Class diagram for a game exploiting specialisation

A: The class diagrams shown are deliberately abstract. We will return to the question of how to build general solutions below, but you might want to reflect now on what would be different in a game of Minesweeper, Noughts-and-Crosses (Tic-Tac-Toe) or Draughts (Chequers). Apart from the multiplicities of some associations, what is changed? Solutions to this activity can be found on the Web site which accompanies this book (details of which were given in the preface).

Of course changing multiplicities is not a trivial matter. As hinted above, different games will have differing numbers of grids, of players and types of tokens. What is adequate for a particular game will not meet all needs. What we can do is to try to push game specific details into specialisations of our abstract classes, but this may need to be reviewed constantly. Bearing this in mind, we will not assume that we have achieved anything like a really flexible design until we have tried it out for a number of examples, where these factors are different.

6.2.3 Modelling Dynamic Behaviour

For the moment we will continue with *Battleships and Cruisers* and look at the game specific behaviour. We start by defining the objects and their links, with the collaboration diagram, shown in figure 6.4.

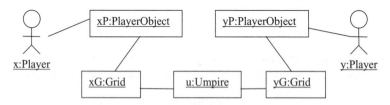

Figure 6.4: Collaboration for *Battleships and Cruisers*

Figure 6.5 shows a possible scenario, consisting of two turns, one by each **Player**, from part of a game, using the example **Grid** shown above for **player X**. This has been produced by a "thought experiment", where the sequence of external actions – messages – was explored by the designers. This particular sequence is typical, but might not occur in any particular game.

In many organisations the Class Responsibility Collaboration (CRC) cards are used to support this phase of development. These are described in detail in several books, and an introduction and additional references can be found in Chapter 2.

By whatever means, it is always very helpful to try to define what you expect to happen in terms of interactions, using either sequence or collaboration diagrams, before moving to considering the internal behaviour of the objects involved. It is important to include the actors in this, since we need to think about how the system will connect to the outside world, and in the UML this is done in terms of the actors involved in use cases.

Q: *Does the interaction shown make the solution any more specific to Battleships and Cruisers? At what point does the specific detail become significant?*

It seems we have got a long way into the problem and are still looking for significant "special-ness" in our problem. Indeed we can go further in building an abstract solution, by seeking to hide more of the features which distinguish this particular game. One intriguing possibility is to integrate the two **Grid** objects, allowing for a composite object which could contain any required number of grids.

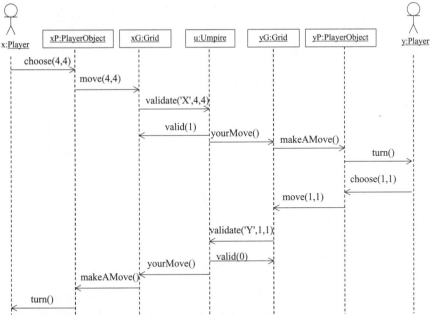

Figure 6.5: Sequence of a scenario from *Battleships and Cruisers*

In the existing solution, grids are allocated one to each **Player**, requiring that the **Umpire** send a message to each in turn, requesting that they prompt their Player to move. The problems of coupling and scaling of the solution both appear in this solution. The **Umpire** is becoming almost a "god class", responsible for everything. The number of grids appears explicitly in the solution, yet we are aware that different games use different numbers of grids. The order of play is explicitly controlled by one object.

The alternative hides the separate **Grid** objects inside a single **GameBoard** object. This encapsulates the detail of how the grids communicate and synchronise knowledge about the game's overall state, particularly whose turn it is next. This needs a revision to the class diagram, but for the moment we simply assume that **GameBoard** aggregates the behaviour of the grids needed and so hides their interactions, so that we can collapse the interaction diagram in line with this. This is a common thing to do when designing a complex system. This implies that the **GameBoard** knows how to decide the order of play, based on the umpire's response.

An example scenario is provided in figure 6.6, which shows objects now interacting with an instance of **GameBoard**.

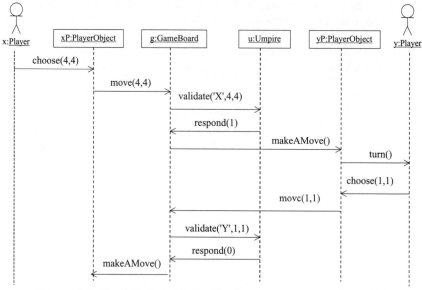

Figure 6.6: Simplified sequence diagram with aggregated Grids

If we move on to consider the internal behaviour of the objects, we might expect to encounter significant specific behaviour for this game, compared to others, at last. Figure 6.7 shows a first view of the statechart of the **GameBoard**.

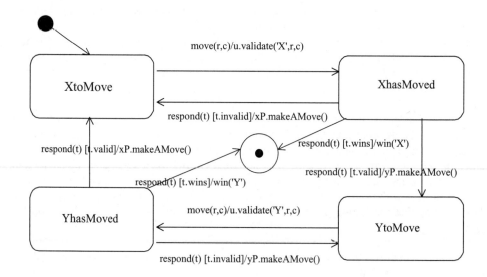

Figure 6.7: Statechart of GameBoard in *Battleships and Cruisers*

The **GameBoard** statechart essentially reflects the overall situation in the game. It describes the progress in terms of moves and outcomes, much as the original description does. Again, there is nothing which is specific to the actual game, apart from the number of *Players* and the order of play. We have left the "business logic", as it is sometimes described, to the **Player** and **Umpire** classes (possible statecharts for these classes are shown in figure 6.8). Some specific work has to be carried out by the **GameBoard**, in order to maintain the flow of information to the **Player** actors, but that can be assumed to take place either in the **makeAMove** operations which are requested or as activities within appropriate states.

Remarkably, even when we describe the internal behaviour of **Player** and **Umpire** objects, we can avoid low level detail, specific to this game, by similar means. The logic shown simply reflects the flow of actions which engage with outside objects. The triggers are all messages invoking operations or the completion of activities within states. These embedded activities are the detailed business logic.

In general this seems to be the best way to use statecharts to represent object-oriented programs. The detailed computation and decision making which defines application specific behaviour tends to overwhelm the expressiveness of these diagrams. Of course, statecharts are defined hierarchically, so that this more specialised logic can be shown within nested states if you wish.

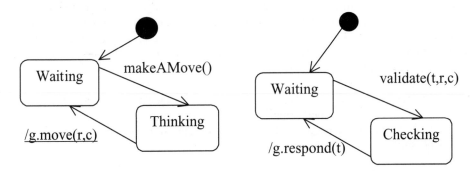

Figure 6.8a: Statechart for *PlayerObject*   Figure 6.8b: Statechart for *Umpire*

You may be wondering about the choice of message type in all of the above. Strictly speaking the interactions have been carried out by asynchronous message passing and this is not the way single threaded programs work, of course. In fact, it doesn't really have to matter, so long as everyone concerned knows what is going on. The **move(r,c)** message sent by a **PlayerObject** may actually be implemented as a returned value from an appropriately typed method in Java. That is really an implementation detail.

6.3   Developing the model further

In this section we are going to take the basic model developed in the previous section and develop some further refinements. These will begin to show how we can take our model of the *Battleships and Cruisers* and provide a more general game framework.

6.3.1 Abstracting to a General Description

So far in this chapter we have built a description of the two-player board game *Battleships and Cruisers*. At each stage we have avoided unnecessarily specific detail and have ended up with a very general framework for two-player games in general. There are still a few specifics in this model however. If we consider these details we find that, by defining a few new abstractions, we can arrive at a far more general solution, which deals with a large class of games. In essence, the specific items left are those which deal with tokens, moves and outcomes.

If we compare *Battleships and Cruisers* with *Noughts and Crosses*, we find that they use different numbers of token types. That can be remedied by defining a generalisation called **Token**.

If we compare both of these games with chequers, we find that the latter needs us to specify both the starting position and the finishing position of the token involved in a move. Again, we can define a suitable generalisation of **Move** as a class.

Finally, we can see that each of the games may have a different set of outcomes from moves, which are required to be reported by the Umpire. Thus, a final generalisation is needed and we have, in fact, done this in the **Umpire**'s statechart, using the name response and an unspecified value. For the sort of logic we have used for **GameBoard**, this would have to contain information on whether a move was valid and on whether it caused the end of the game, as a win or a draw.

A: Some games have situations where the next player is selected according to the move made. This may mean a player skipping a turn or the order of play (in games with more than two players) being reversed. Try to redesign the **GameBoard** class to allow for these possibilities.

6.3.2 Expressing a Complete Behavioural Model

Once we have a model of both the external behaviour (interaction diagrams) and internal behaviour (statechart) of a system, we work to check their consistency. This can be done in a number of ways, but a useful aid is to draw the combined collaboration and statechart diagram for the system. In very complex systems it may be necessary to do this either for sub-systems or at high levels of abstraction, in order to manage complexity, but it is generally useful. Figure 6.9 shows a high level model of overall behaviour in the *Battleships and Cruisers* example. Unfortunately no CASE tool that we know of supports such a combined model.

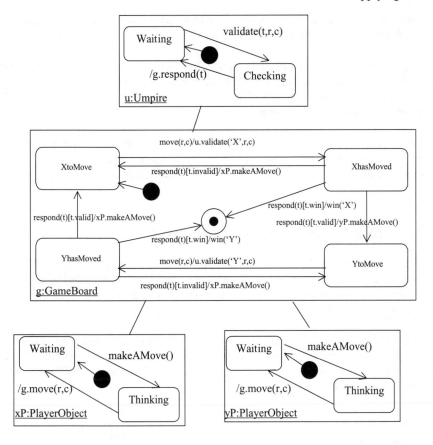

Figure 6.9: Combined statechart and collaboration diagram for a game

Using this diagram we can explore how the system will behave, starting by placing a small counter or coin on the start states of the four objects. We then move one of these markers to start the game's logic.

In this case all four objects will move from their initial states (their filled black discs) before anything else happens. We could choose to interpret the order in which we allow this to happen to indicate a sequence of object generation, or even that one object creates another as part of its constructor sequence.

That will give an overall situation where the **Umpire** is **Waiting**, each **PlayerObject** is **Waiting** and the **GameBoard** is in the **XtoMove** state. The only transition which can fire is within the **GameBoard**, from the **XtoMove** to the **XhasMoved** state, causing a **makeAMove** message to be sent to **PlayerObject**, **xP**. The **makeAMove** message causes **xP** to move to the **Thinking** state and so we move that marker as well.

From that situation the next transition has to be to where **xP** sends a move message back to the **GameBoard**, returning itself to the **Waiting** state.

Following the chain of events will show us how the logic we have defined causes messages to be interchanged and so validate the scenario. In this model we have more than one path, shown as alternative transitions out of some states. Each represents a new scenario and depends on input values to the system.

 A: Carry through with this validation and compare the message sequences with those expected from the message sequence chart shown earlier, adapted to this generic view. Does the behaviour match that required for the game to work?

6.3.3 A Completely Abstract Framework

It is, of course, never possible to assume that any solution is completely general. You may well know several games that could not be accommodated within the solution we have now reached. What we have to try to ensure is that nothing that fits the general problem area we have to deal with can take us by surprise.

Figure 6.10 shows the class diagram for a proposed abstract framework. Only **GameBoard** can be fleshed out in any detail and even that probably depends on assumptions which are quite narrow. Most of the rest consists of «interface» definitions for **Player, Umpire, Move, Response** and **Token**.

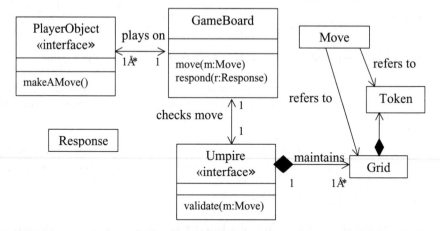

Figure 6.10: Class diagram for abstract game framework

Note that in the above class diagram, the **Response** class has no associations with other classes. The **Response** and **Move** classes are both shown as parameters to operations defined in the **GameBoard** class. We could (for completeness) add associations to the **Response**, but the point is that this might be seen to clutter the diagram, and it is not always necessary to add every detailed association. There is an element of judgement on the part of the modeller to balance what is appropriate to show versus what might be strictly correct in terms of the notation being used.

In creating this final version of our design, one issue cropped up which had been unseen previously. How can it be that the **GameBoard** updates the grids yet the **Umpire** is able to validate moves against them? We could, of course, add one or more access operations, allowing the Umpire to interrogate the **GameBoard** about the current state of the *grids*. This would be sensible if the **GameBoard** ever did anything which required it to have independent access to the grids, but it turns out that it does not. Following the principle of Occam's razor (which basically says when presented with a number of alternatives, any of which will do, then always choose the simplest), we redefine the associations in the class diagram, making the **Grid** objects part of the **Umpire** class.

6.3.4 Communication with the User

We now need to see how this system would communicate with a user. In any game of the type we are considering, this can be thought of as having two parts.

1. We need to be able to display the appropriate **Grid** to the corresponding player.

2. We need to be able to send messages to players.

To solve the first of these we can exploit a similar form of abstraction, based on generalisation, to that we used to create a general game framework. By defining an abstract **drawGrid** operation within the **Grid** class we provide the simplest solution. When implementing the game, this would have an appropriate method defined in a specialisation, which uses the desired package for display.

A more elaborate solution would define a **GridImage** class to which update and display requests could be sent. A number of specialisations of this could be provided, to suit different output possibilities. This might seem redundant, but would allow a single implementation, which could decide what form of object, and therefore interaction, to create when starting up.

For the second, we can similarly add an abstract method, **displayMessage** to the **Player** class or build a message display class.

6.3.5 Deploying the Game's Elements

If the game is to run on a single machine, we have no deployment problems to solve. Messages are passed using method invocations in Java or whatever is equivalent in the implementation language used. We can use something like the Thread library of Java to simulate asynchronous behaviour, but there is no genuine concurrency if everything is sharing a single processor.

If the game is to run over a network, performance problems become more interesting. We have to choose where the various elements are to be deployed and, based on this, decide which associations correspond to remote message passing, at least in principle. UML provides deployment diagrams to help with this and figure 6.11 gives a suggestion of how the game framework could be mapped in this way.

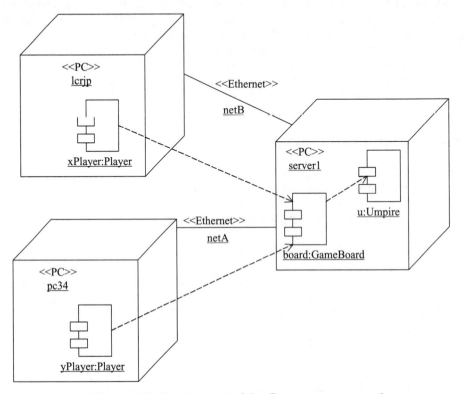

Figure 6.11: Deployment of the Game over a network

Whenever we simply show a link between communicating objects as an association, we are abstracting away from the physical realisation of that communication. In a deployment diagram we show physical links between nodes and logical links between components. The combination of these two must match the dependencies between component types.

The simplest view to take is that a component matches some high level object, which is capable of partial autonomy. The dependencies are the associations between these objects and the physical links define the characteristics of these associations when they are instantiated.

By examining the physical characteristics of links and nodes and matching these to the expected requirements of the components we can estimate the performance of the application when deployed this way. Although we may lack sufficient information to make an accurate estimate, we can look for bottlenecks and warn users where this might cause problems.

6.4   Summary and discussion

This model was chosen so that we could explore notions of reuse and abstraction. We have observed that low coupling, through minimisation of message passing dependencies, may not be achievable. Nevertheless we have found that abstraction, exploiting UML's generalisation mechanisms, provides an alternative path to reuse.

Such a view of systems is equivalent to that used in many design patterns or frameworks. The result is, arguably, a game logic pattern which can be reused either as a design starting point or, more concretely, as a library of abstract classes and interfaces in a suitable language, such as Java. Java versions of both this framework and some games built with it are available from our Web site.

We have also explored how to separate the core (business) logic of an application from its user interface. What is clear is that a similar approach can be used, using an abstract target for input and output requests. These abstract targets can then be provided with appropriate specialisations to embed the application within a particular environment.

Further reading

There aren't any specific readings that we would like to associate with this case study. If there are points concerning the use of notation that you are unfamiliar with at this stage we would recommend that you revisit Chapter 2. Hopefully that chapter, and its associated further readings will help to address some, if not all, of your queries.

7

Road Junction

The focus for this case study will be on a traffic light control system. It addresses a realtime engineering level problem, where synchronisation and timing are significant aspects of the requirements. It is a considerable simplification, in many ways, and for a realistic example of this sort of problem you might like to look at a paper by David Harel, the originator of statecharts, which is in the list of further reading at the end of this chapter.

The case study focusses on the detail of states, interactions and system testing. In addition to the core UML features you are probably familiar with by now, it uses concepts and elements introduced in the recent proposal for a *Profile for Schedulability, Performance and Time* (previously mentioned in Chapter 3). These points are summarised in the following *UML Used in this Chapter* information box.

UML Used in this Chapter	USE CASE DIAGRAM	to examine and capture requirements.
	STATECHART	to illustrate the internal behaviour of objects in both software and hardware.
	CLASS DIAGRAM	to examine system structure.
	INTERACTION DIAGRAM	to express system dynamics.
	PROFILE FOR SCHEDULABILITY, PERFORMANCE AND TIME	to express timing dependencies.

There is an emphasis in many UML case studies on the structure and the types of object used in the design. What is different about the following example is that it deals with the importance in many examples of a focus on understanding system dynamics. The external dynamic behaviour is shown in case studies where sequence, interaction and activity diagrams are used. What these do not show is the importance of the internal behaviour of the objects and how this can change the way they will react to messages in the future. For a design to be complete it must take both internal and external behaviour into account.

Another important aspect of design which we have not covered in our other case studies is the hardware/software interface. In embedded systems there may well be hardware components which carry out some of the functions required. These can be modelled as UML objects, even though they are not written as parts of a program. This allows us to design the software and the hardware together, a process often referred to as *software-hardware co-design*.

Finally, many systems have real time aspects to them. This means that they are sensitive to the time taken for a response to some message or may require a reaction within a given time delay. To capture these features we need to look more deeply at how we model certain aspects of systems in the UML. We must also find ways to analyse this information, so that we can determine whether our UML design meets the required standards.

7.1 Case study introduction

There are three distinct problems to be dealt with for this case study. First we need ways of representing timed behaviour, second we need to be able to determine whether the delays in the system disrupt the logical behaviour of that system, third we need to be able to estimate the magnitude of those delays in comparison to the system's requirements. This will perhaps make you look at traffic lights in a whole new way! A description of the system is provided in figure 7.1

We are asked to design a system to control the traffic lights at a road junction. Lights are set to one or more colours, which determine what cars may do. The lights must ensure a smooth flow of traffic and offer pedestrians a safe opportunity to cross the roads meeting at the junction.

Each combination of colours permits different actions for cars approaching it.

Red means "stop".

Green means "carry on" or "start moving".

Amber means "slow down, ready to stop".

Red and amber together mean "get ready to move off".

The lights change according to the following rules:

- if the lights have not changed for 90 seconds they move through the sequence from green to red, via red and amber, or from red to green, via amber

- if there are cars approaching or waiting at a red light and no cars approaching the green light, the change sequence occurs

- if a pedestrian pushes the crossing button on a light, the change sequence occurs if that light was on green

---

Figure 7.1: Case study description

A: Work through the description given above in figure 7.1. Convince yourself that you understand it and see if you agree that it describes a traffic light fully and accurately. As in previous case study chapters, think about initial use cases and actors, as well as possible candidate objects and classes. You will be able to compare your own ideas with those we present throughout this chapter.

7.2 Application of UML

There is one important aspect of this particular example, which causes us to look for new solutions. The problem supposes a junction with a number of roads meeting. Since these roads have to be controlled in a synchronised manner, it has significant real time aspects.

- How do we ensure that the lights are not merely following their individual sequences, but that these sequences are in time with each other?

- How do we ensure the safety of both cars and pedestrians?

For the purposes of this chapter we will restrict our initial discussion to a classic cross-roads, which is shown in figure 7.2. Each of the four roads which meets at the junction requires its own traffic light, which must work together with the others.

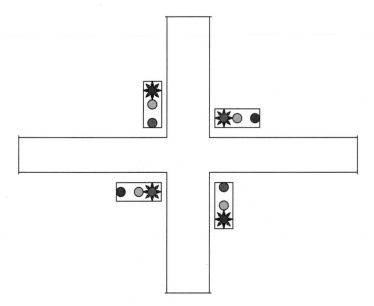

Figure 7.2: Layout of example junction

The timing of changes of lights has very important consequences, since both drivers and pedestrians need to be able to gain safe passage across the junction. The overall state of the junction, which is made up of the combination of the states of the individual lights and any cars and pedestrians currently present, has to maintain both progress and safety. If lights become out of synchronisation, safety will be compromised. If combinations allowing progress for both cars and pedestrians cannot be achieved repeatedly, the system fails.

We may also need to consider whether the time available to cars and pedestrians to complete their crossing of the junction is adequate.

There is a further set of questions, which deal with what will happen if the lights fail in some way. These represent alternative scenarios to be addressed. In all cases there is a very strong need for the system to fail safely, i.e. for any failure to result in a combination of light states which is not dangerous to users. Although these are crucial, we do not have space to deal with them here. Basically, any failure should leave all lights set to red.

7.2.1 Use Case Model

There seem to be two actors in our traffic light example. The **Driver** and **Pedestrian** actors stand for those who cross the junction *on* a road and those who cross the junction *across* a road, respectively. We can use the use case model to express time requirements, if we wish. Thus a pedestrian might need a minimum of ten seconds to complete crossing the road.

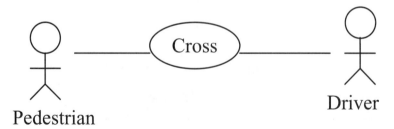

Figure 7.3: Use case model of a junction

Q: *Are both of the actors identified in this model really actors in the way you understand? What is the means by which each of them can initiate the use case and what is the benefit they gain from it? Consider this question at this point before moving on, as we will discuss this in the following text.*

It may be that your initial use case diagram had only a single actor, possibly the **Pedestrian**. This is our experience when using this case study in teaching activities. This is an exercise to establish an agreed system scope. Are we purely going to focus our attention on the pedestrians who want to cross the junction, or do we also care about the effect of the system operation on the vehicle drivers? We would argue that both actors derive benefit from the use case, as they both want to cross the junction.

7.2.2 Class Model

We need to develop a set of components from which the traffic light system can be constructed. As usual, this is done by defining a class diagram, with appropriate associations, operations etc.

There have been several proposals for mechanisms to incorporate time in the UML, but we will start by assuming that there is a class called Timer which can send synchronising messages to the other classes in an application. This is shown as having the stereotype «RTtimer», which is one of the features of the *UML Profile for Schedulability, Performance and Time*. For simplicity we will simply refer to this as the Profile from now on. This profile will not provide a complete solution, but it will enable us to explore possible answers and to expose the underlying questions we have to address.

Figure 7.4 provides a brief summary of the aspects of the Profile which we are using, especially **RTtimer** and **RTtimeout**. Essentially we will define a class **Timer** as derived from the stereotype **RTtimer** and a signal, **Timeout**, based on **RTtimeout**. There is a slightly more extensive coverage of this profile in Appendix A.

Timer will by definition have a duration, which can be set as a constraint, and be able to send **Timeout** signals when this duration has completed. In so doing, we potentially open the model to analysis by appropriate tools, which can interpret the profile's stereotypes, tags and constraints as having the same meaning as we are using.

Figure 7.4a shows how the formal definition of these key elements is built up using the UML extension mechanisms. Figure 7.4b shows these elements within the sort of class diagram we are used to building for ourselves. Essentially we have two forma of timing mechanism, Clock and Timer. Each of these has certain key attributes and operations, most of which come from their parent class, **TimingMechanism**. **Clock** can generate **ClockInterrupt** signals, while **Timer** can generate **Timeout** signals. We will explore the features of **Timer** further as we use them in our model.

You will notice that the list of tags in the stereotype definition is not the same as the elements within the classes in the second view. This reflects the draft nature of the profile at the time of writing. It is not important for our purposes, but you may want to check the current definition when you read this, for a more consistent view.

The key features of **Timer** which we will need to use are its **duration**, which determines the period after which it sends a **Timeout** and the **isPeriodic** flag, which makes it send repeatedly each time duration elapses.

In some ways a **Timer** is a more explicit way of representing the **after()** trigger, but it can (and in this example will) be extended, to provide more complex behaviour than a simple time delay.

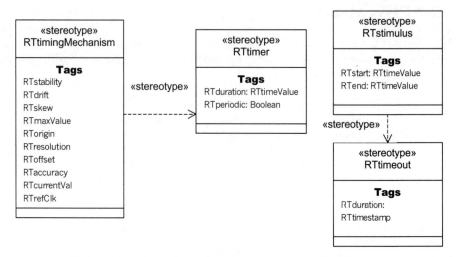

Figure 7.4a: Some key stereotypes within the Profile

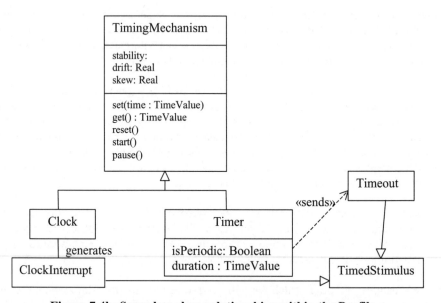

Figure 7.4b: Some key class relationships within the Profile

Using these elements as our components, we arrive at figure 7.5. In particular, you should note the **reset()** operation in **Timer**. This appears in some places in the profile, but not consistently. We include it as an additional feature, which resets the internal counter to zero. This counter is **RTcurrentVal**, which also appears in some parts of the profile but not in others. We assume that this records the time that has passed since the last **reset**, until **duration** is reached, when the **Timer** resets itself.

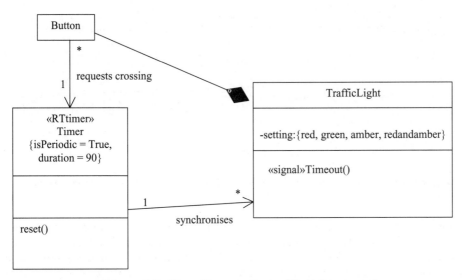

Figure 7.5: Class diagram for traffic light example

7.2.3 Interaction Diagrams

The traffic light control problem seems like a classic for a set of sequence diagrams to describe its scenarios. It has some particular problems, however, which make it hard to represent without some forms of extension.

Consider figure 7.6, where we describe a **Pedestrian** pushing **Button b1**. According to the description we are working from, if **TrafficLight t1** is currently green, the change sequence is initiated. We consider that scenario in what follows.

We might simply allow the **Button** to send a message to each **TrafficLight** object, starting the change. In a system where timing and synchronisation are not significant, that would work adequately. Unfortunately the scenario we wish to describe is not free of such constraints and we must deal with them.

Q: *What might happen if we allowed the Button to force the TrafficLights to change* *without involving the timer? Put yourself in the Pedestrian's position to see why that would be a bad choice. The messages to the TrafficLights are shown as synchronous. What implications does that have for our model? This question will be discussed in the text as you read on.*

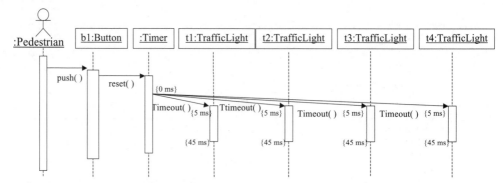

Figure 7.6: Typical sequence diagram for junction – pedestrian crosses road successfully

The **Timer** receives a **reset()** message from the **Button**. This is a standard operation for any class based on the **RTtimer** stereotype. It resets the **Timer** to its initial state, i.e. it starts it counting elapsed time from zero again. We assume that our particular timer also sends signals to each of the four **TrafficLights** in response to the reset message, forcing them to change. These messages will be of a special stereotype known as **Timeout** signals, in the **Profile**.

The need to reset the **Timer** whenever a pedestrian request causes the lights to change is crucial. If it did not happen that way, the **Timer** would force another change at the end of whatever remained of its timing interval. The consequences for the pedestrian could be catastrophic!

A further problem which we really should face up to is how to force all four lights to change simultaneously. Even if we ignore the possibility that one light's **Timeout()** might fail to arrive, due to faulty wiring, we certainly do not want one light to change even a short time before or after the others. The sequence diagram in figure 7.7 sidesteps this issue by making the four **TrafficLights** into a single **Junction** object. This disguises the problem, however, rather than solving it.

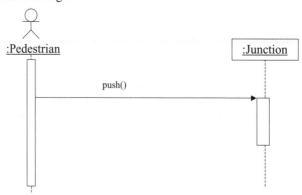

Figure 7.7: High level view of the same scenario

In the model given (referring back to the sequence diagram in figure 7.6), the timing information is shown using timing marks. These are written as constraints inside braces, indicating the time at which events should happen. We see that the **Timeout()** messages are all sent at time 0. This is chosen arbitrarily, since we want merely to show the elapsed time before each successive event which results. We note that all the messages are assumed to take 5 ms to arrive, which triggers the action sequence in each **TrafficLight** (shown by the overlaid rectangle on their lifeline). This sequence then completes after a further 40 ms.

As always, we can use the equivalent collaboration view of the same sequence of interactions, where we can use letters within the numbering scheme to show that certain messages are concurrent. Thus, in figure 7.8 the initial **push()** is numbered 1, the resulting **reset()** is 1.1. The resulting **Timeout()** signals are numbered 1.1.1a, b, c and d, where the extra digit indicates that they all result from message 1.1 and the use of the same digit followed by letters indicates that they can be executed in any order or concurrently. This does not show the timing requirements given in the sequence diagram, however. In general it is more messy to annotate collaborations in that way.

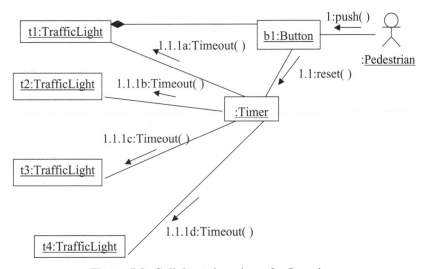

Figure 7.8: Collaboration view of a Junction

Figure 7.9 shows the same high level view of a single Junction object as did Figure 7.7, but this time as a collaboration.

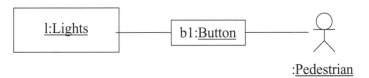

Figure 7.9: High level view of a Junction

7.2.4 Statecharts

The sequence diagram shows how the objects and actors need to interact to allow the Junction to function. What is now needed is a picture of how the internal logic of these objects works to deliver this behaviour. In particular, we need to know that all possibilities are correctly handled.

Figure 7.10 shows a possible statechart for a **TrafficLight**. It has four main states and moves in turn through these, representing the sequence specified in the problem statement. The trigger for each transition is either a **Timeout()** signal or the lapsing of a period since the last change. We can use this simple model to examine whether such a description is adequate.

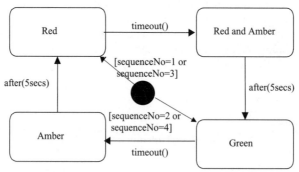

7.10: Statechart for a TrafficLight

Since this is a general description of all our lights, we show two possible transitions from the initial state, corresponding to the need to set two lights to red and two to green initially. We express this by a guard which checks a property, **sequenceNumber**, set in the object's generation.

Figure 7.11a shows a description of our **Timer** class. It is a specialisation of a generic Timer class from the Profile. We introduce our own special method for the predefined operation reset(). This sends a **Timeout()** signal to each of the 4 lights before resetting its timing counter to zero. We also show a periodic sending of 4 **Timeout()** signals, followed by resetting the counter, based on an interval set as a property of the tag duration when the object is created.

Figure 7.11b shows the same behaviour, but with a distinguished state for the period where the **Timer** is sending its **Timeout()** signals. This may seem unnecessary, but will be important when we look at the states of the overall system, below.

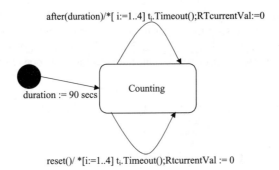

after(duration)/*[i:=1..4] t_j.Timeout();RTcurrentVal:=0

duration := 90 secs

Counting

reset()/ *[i:=1..4] t_i.Timeout();RtcurrentVal := 0

7.11a: Statechart for our Timer

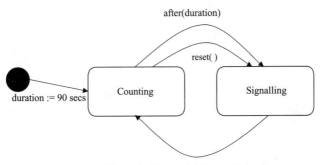

after(duration)

reset( )

duration := 90 secs

Counting

Signalling

/*[i:=1..4] t_i.Timeout();RTcurrentVal := 0

7.11b: Alternative statechart for our Timer

7.2.5 Further Timing Details

This example raises several important issues, which recur in similar cases where control and synchronisation are essential to the requirements. We have addressed the specification of timing constraints by annotating those sequence diagrams which show the expected behaviour of the system. If we collect all the scenarios which are possible, we can check that they are both mutually consistent and cover all the cases we have identified in our use case model. This, however, assumes that we have understood all the possible cases and that we have adequate techniques for this checking to take place.

The internal behaviour of the system's components is defined in the statecharts we created for them. In order to ensure that they support the required external interactions, as shown in the sequence diagrams, they must be checked in response to all sequences of messages which make up these scenarios.

If we want to see an overall view of this behaviour, we can combine the collaboration diagram (external view) and the statechart (internal view), giving a full model. Figure 7.12 shows how this would look.

We can now choose an initial combination of states for the objects and examine how that model would develop following the scenarios we showed in our sequence diagrams. Table 7.1 shows the initial setting of lights 1 and 3 to red with 2 and 4 to green. This is then allowed to unfold without any pedestrian intervention for one full cycle, apparently returning to its initial state.

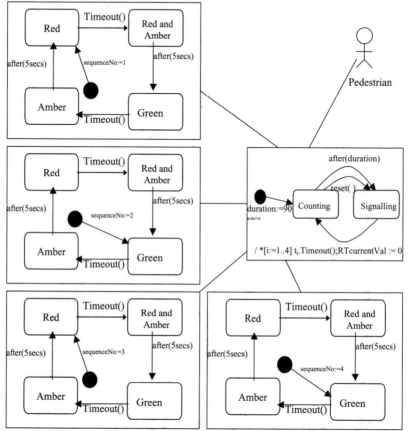

Figure 7.12: Combined Statechart and Collaboration diagram for Junction

State	Time	Light number				
No.	secs	1	2	3	4	Timer
1	0	red	green	red	green	Counting
2	90	red	green	red	green	Signalling
3	90	red & amber	amber	red & amber	amber	Counting
4	95	green	red	green	red	Counting
5	180	green	red	green	red	Signalling
6	180	amber	red & amber	amber	red & amber	Signalling
1	185	red	green	red	green	Counting

Table 7.1: State sequence for lights only

An alternative way of showing such a sequence is to draw a statechart. Each row of the table corresponds to one possible state of the whole system. Note that the name of each state in this diagram refers to a state number in table 7.1. In this example the resulting diagram is a cyclical directed graph. Each node of the graph, as shown in figure 7.13, is a state and each edge is the event, which leads to the change. In this case most of the events are passing of fixed intervals of time. Some events are synchronisation messages, however, in the form of **Timeout()** signals.

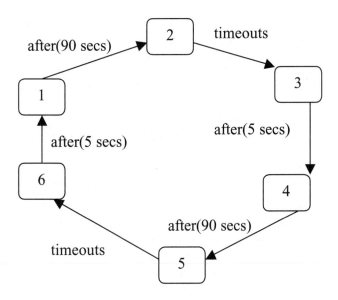

Figure 7.13: High level state transition diagram of junction

However, this picture is really deceptive, since the time intervals of 5 and 90 seconds may actually overlap; it fails to take account of a subtle difference in the state of the Timer on the two occasions when the system returns to the original set of colours. To see this we need to include the current value of **RTcurrentval** as part of the state information for **Timer**.

Table 7.2 shows this and we can immediately see that the **Timer** has counted 5 when the overall system returns to the initial colours. If we follow this through, we discover that from state 9 in table 7.2 the sequence repeats an eight state sequence, from 2 to 8, indefinitely. It is only the initial sequence that is different and the only significant difference is that state 1 lasts 5 seconds longer than state 9.

Such a small difference in the initial sequence's timing might be unimportant, but it is just such small differences which can make a system fail.

State No.	Time secs	Light number				Timer
		1	2	3	4	
1	0	red	green	red	green	Counting, 0
2	90	red	green	red	green	Signalling, 90
3	90	red & amber	amber	red & amber	amber	Signalling, 0
4	90	red & amber	amber	red & amber	amber	Counting, 0
5	95	green	red	green	red	Counting, 5
6	180	green	red	green	red	Signalling, 90
7	180	amber	red & amber	amber	red & amber	Signalling, 0
8	180	amber	red & amber	amber	red & amber	Counting, 0
9	185	red	green	red	green	Counting, 5

Table 7.2: State sequence for lights with time for Timer

A: Draw the statechart for the system as shown in table 7.2. Now try to define a modified model which would ensure that the period spent in the initial state is the same as that spent in each equivalent later state.

Clearly the slight irregularity identified above is not significant. It does, however, show how even an apparently simple system can be much more difficult to describe accurately than appears true at first sight. Even without pedestrians and monitoring of waiting cars, the system repays some analysis of its timed behaviour. What difference would it make if a pedestrian could push a button and trigger a change of lights?

It is actually quite easy to see in this case that the only difference is that the system behaves in an identical fashion, except that the period of 85 seconds between lights reaching one of the red/green states, i.e. state 5 or state 9 in table 7.2, and the next **Timeout()** messages being sent could now be any interval from zero to 85 seconds.

7.3 Summary and discussion

This example has been used to illustrate a few of the problems we encounter when we try to express systems with time related behaviour and requirements in the UML. Although the logic of the traffic lights is quite simple, they illustrate how tricky it can be to capture such aspects.

Perhaps the most important addition to our modelling is the use of state transition diagrams, which are not part of the UML, but are a traditional part of system design, to examine the behaviour of the system as a whole. In this case we have used fixed (deterministic) timings and examined the scheduling of events within the system.

Sequence and collaboration diagrams let us express the desired (or required) sequence and any time constraints on these.

Combined statechart and collaboration diagrams let us generate the overall behaviour generated by the logic of the statecharts of the individual objects in the system. Building on this we can derive the overall state transition diagrams of the system and the resulting event sequences, to match against those required.

Adding timings to the model allows us to check the response times etc., either deterministically or as bounds or averages.

Further reading

The following is a useful reference if you would like to read further about the original statechart usage described by David Harel:

> Harel, D., Drusinsky, D., *Using statecharts for hardware description and synthesis*, IEEE Transactions on Computer Aided Design, 1989.

8

Supporting Distributed Working

This chapter introduces the final of our four core case studies in Part Two. It takes a slightly different form to the other previous three case studies and hopefully you will find it a refreshing and interesting read. This chapter is based on our own experiences in applying UML in a medium scale distributed project where the project team members are geographically spread. Let's think about that for a moment. By medium scale, there were six different partner groups, with each of these groups having an average of around eight different people engaged in the project at various times and in various roles. The other important thing to know about this work is that the partner groups were in different countries, which added an interesting cross-cultural element to our working.

This case study concerns the importance of supporting communication between people in a project. The communication of ideas and concepts between people can be difficult enough if people are in the same building. If we introduce geographical and cultural boundaries then these difficulties are magnified. Communication is at the heart of why we use UML to support our modelling activities. Modelling is about understanding a problem or situation and communicating that effectively to other people – often so that we can agree that the problem and/or solution are agreed and understood. So, isn't this what we've been doing through the previous case studies in looking at UML notation to capture requirements and describe dynamic behaviour of systems? Well, yes. But how are these diagrams actually produced? By a single person locked away in a room – or a group of people working collectively? These are the kinds of things that we will be looking at in this chapter, and giving some actual examples from our experience in the project that we will describe. Through this case study we will introduce and explore the following:

- Exploring the different circumstances and situations under which UML can be applied. For example, dynamic usage during meetings and more static usage where documented concepts and ideas are circulated amongst the project members.

- We will examine *scenarios of usage*. This will consider what these are, and why they are important. In particular, examining the role that modelling can play in a distributed working environment and the ways in which modelling activities can occur.

- Highlighting the difficulties in presenting and disseminating UML diagrams. If you have a model of even medium complexity resulting in a diagram of a certain size, how can that model be presented in an effective manner to people in a distributed environment?

The project on which this case study is based is something that we were personally involved with, so our report is of first hand experiences. This case study examines how UML can be used to support interpersonal communication and clarification of problems and design solutions in order to agree a way forward in the project. This is important as it moves us away from looking purely at how UML can support a traditional view of requirements, analysis, design and implementation – we use it as a vehicle to support and clarify the way that people work. We are looking more here at modelling *processes* and how UML can be used.

Chapter 4 discussed the importance of process in a general sense. The subject will be raised again in Part Three of this book where we consider the Capability Maturity Model (CMM) as a framework for comparing and evaluating different methodologies/process models. We are not going to dwell on the subject of processes in detail here, but we would like to identify a number of separate problem areas and consider in what ways UML can help us.

We can consider that the majority of process models and methodologies that apply to projects will comprise analysis, design and implementation phases or stages that work will progress through. We can loosely define these as a number of *problem areas* as illustrated in figure 8.1 where we require notations and techniques to support our work. Whilst we can identify and talk about these problem areas it is better to consider some continuity of flow between them – for this reason they are shown with a degree of overlap in the diagram.

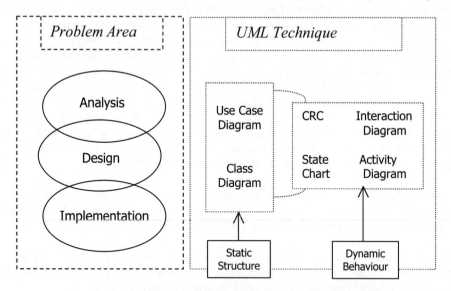

Figure 8.1 Application of UML to traditional lifecycle

We can then consider a general mapping of UML to these problem areas. The static structure diagrams (use case and class diagrams) are shown as being broadly helpful across all three of the problem areas, helping clarify outline ideas and requirements during analysis, through design and into implementation. It is particularly important that we move away from thinking about class diagrams in terms of modelling at the software implementation level only, and hopefully the previous case studies have made this point. The diagrams that support modelling of dynamic behaviour supplement the modelling activities by helping to clarify, elaborate and test the static structure models. Note that in the following diagram we include the Class Responsibility Collaboration (CRC). Whilst the CRC card technique is not part of UML it is still a helpful and complimentary technique to consider in modelling dynamic behaviour and checking or developing static models. Many helpful references to CRC cards can be found, but as an introduction consider the *Using UML* text by Stevens and Pooley (see the *Further reading* section of Chapter 2 for further details).

When most people think about applying UML it is with such problem areas in mind. Asking questions along the lines of "how do we use use-case or class diagrams to support requirements capture during analysis". This case study will allow us to take a subtly different view – that of using UML to support people more directly in the project, so as more of a vehicle for communication than specification or documentation. This distinction perhaps seems a little too subtle at this stage, so see what you think after reviewing this case study.

The project on which this case study is based is itself interesting as it concerns the development of an architecture/framework to support distributed software development. The project will be outlined further in the following section. This case study will focus on UML elements summarised in the following *UML Used in this Chapter* information box.

UML Used in this Chaper	**USE CASE DIAGRAM**	to examine the scope of the system – or part of the system under examination.
	INTERACTION DIAGRAM	to express system dynamics and act as sanity check on design solutions during meetings.
	ACTIVITY DIAGRAM	a key tool used to explore scenarios of usage.
	IMPLEMENTATION DIAGRAM	to illustrate the developing architecture and deployment of modules and functionality across a number of nodes.
	CLASS DIAGRAM	to illustrate the developing architecture/framework.

8.1 Case study introduction

System modellers and software developers would tend to agree that distributed software development is complex. The complexity increases with the number of partners you have in a project, and the range of geography and culture that separate them.

The OPHELIA (Open Platform and meTHodologies for deVELopment tools and IntegrAtion in a distributed environment) project is a European Union funded initiative that aims to develop a platform to support software engineering in a distributed environment.

The project is due for completion towards the end of 2003. The project involves the design and implementation of an infrastructure to support distributed software design and development. The OPHELIA infrastructure aims to support the plugin of a range of existing commercial and open source tools through a common interface. The infrastructure will support the exchange of data between the tools connected to the environment. The infrastructure also comes with an integration layer. This provides a range of added value services to support traceability and event notification between project artefacts.

The OPHELIA project involves partners in six different geographical locations and cultures; Spain, Italy, Czech Republic, Poland, Germany and the United Kingdom. The project then presents us with the difficulties that the project itself aims to address, namely how can we enable people who are so geographically and culturally spread to work in a productive manner? To a large extent this involves understanding work practices, as we shall see. The aim of this case study is to show the ways in which UML can be applied to help address some of these difficulties.

The OPHELIA project is typical of many EU projects whereby a number of geographically separate partners work towards some common project goal. The underlying work is divided into a number of workpackages. In the case of the OPHELIA project we had, for example, a modelling module workpackage, a metrics module workpackage, a requirements module workpackage etc. Each of these workpackages represents a typical category of tool that we would want to plug into the distributed architecture. Two partner organisations in the project represent our customer base, and as such are responsible for developing a set of requirements. Other partners can then also contribute to this. A key component of the infrastructure is the support for traceability of objects across tools supported within the OPHELIA framework. This represents the added value of linking a number of tools into OPHELIA.

As fascinating as the OPHELIA project is, this case study is not about the project itself *per se*. This case study concerns our experiences in applying UML within the project where we encountered a number of communication difficulties.

8.2 Application of UML

The day to day work on the project was fairly informal, with each partner able to adopt their own work practices. We worked without a formally adopted or agreed methodology, beyond the accepted norm for a project such as this where the work is research based and of an exploratory nature, therefore inevitably involving many prototyping efforts to test and evaluate technologies and approaches.

Table 8.1 provides a summary of UML diagrams and the purpose to which they were used in the OPHELIA project (not all of which are represented in this chapter). This clearly shows the use of notation, but also the different ways in which it was used.

Note that we make distinctions between formal and informal documentation. By documentation we mean that some UML diagrams were recorded and accompanying text was added to form some document. Examples would be a requirements document, a technical specification or end user documentation. The documentation may be *formal* in that it is recorded and circulated amongst partners through a central repository, and at times published outside of the project group (conferences, journals for example). The *informal* documentation tended to be more local and not shared with other project members. This tended to be more disposable documentation, which served a purpose but would be unlikely to be referred to at a later stage in the project. If this were to be the case then an informal document would be reclassified as a formal document.

	Formal documentation	Informal document	Presentation	Dynamic meeting	Web publishing
Use Case diagram	✓				✓
Class diagram	✓	✓		✓	✓
Interaction diagram	✓	✓	✓	✓	
Implementation diagram	✓	✓	✓	✓	
Package diagram	✓				✓
Activity diagram	✓		✓		✓

Table 8.1: Summary of UML usage

The use of UML diagrams in documentation is something that typically comes to mind when you think about how a diagram will be used. In many ways you may find that the other uses listed in table 8.1 are a little more interesting or unusual. Certain UML diagrams were developed purely for presentations. These were typically either very high level overview diagrams or detailed and focussed sub-diagrams that made some overall point for clarity and explanation. Diagrams were also often developed as part of a meeting, sometimes in formal technical meetings and sometimes less formal brain-storming sessions. These may be disposable forms of UML, in that the diagram was not recorded or referred to after the meeting (since it had served its purpose). At other times the diagram may be developed further after the meeting and find its way into a formal or informal document. The final use indicated in table 8.1 concerns web publishing of diagrams and models. This is becoming an increasingly used and useful means to disseminate information.

We could have added more categories of use of UML (for example we could identify formal and informal presentations), but those included in table 8.1 provide a reasonable representation of our core applications in the OPHELIA project. They will be elaborated on further in the following subsections.

8.2.1 Exploring Uses of UML

The project saw us using UML in a number of different ways. We can broadly refer to these as *informal* and *formal* forms of usage. The formal applications of UML are instances where models were developed and recorded formally. Such models become a recorded artefact of the project. The model would often be recorded in a UML modelling tool, though this was not mandatory. At times it would be more appropriate to record diagrams directly into documents and presentation files (i.e. using drawing capabilities outside of the formal modelling tool such as those provided by Word or Powerpoint). This might have been done for a variety of reasons, but was most typically because the diagram was either very simple and recording in the UML tool would have been cumbersome, or at times because the diagram could not be adequately supported by the tool. Examples of these latter diagrams are the implementation diagrams that are not well supported in UML tools.

We shall begin with an examination of what we consider to be the more effective ways in which UML was applied, though later on we will discuss the implications of less effective uses just to show that we are also human!

Formal applications of UML

The project mostly made use of use case and class diagrams to define user requirements and module interfaces. These models were recorded in UML modelling tools and incorporated into formal project documents and presentations.

The project also made good use of implementation diagrams, incorporating both node and deployment details. It can often be difficult for people learning about UML to really see a necessary application for the implementation diagrams. They proved invaluable in the context of this project where we were exploring the impact of a distributed software environment. It was essential that we could identify and explore the software components, their physical deployment and the means by which they would communicate. This was especially relevant since there was uncertainty about a degree of the technology to be used, particularly the role of CORBA. CORBA was a technology that was not well known to all developers and technical designers – it was important that we found a means to see the role that it would play in the developing project architecture

Understanding the implications of CORBA was therefore identified as a key concern of the project and the way in which the developing software solution would work. UML helped project partners in clarifying the role that this technology would play. The diagram in figure 8.2 is a typical example from the OPHELIA project. This was used as a diagram exchanged between partners and was therefore primarily supporting internal project communication. Such diagrams were also subsequently used in formal publications and presentations to explain an implementation of the OPHELIA architecture.

The diagram shows three potential nodes, each with a number of separate software components. Communication paths between software components are clearly represented, as is the access to information via CORBA interfaces. This diagram made the use of interfaces explicit as well as the communication links (i.e. which software components could communicate with which other components). Each partner was working on a different tool, and agreeing on how these tools would interact was of primary importance in the project. The implementation diagram was essential in helping technical solutions teams to express ideas to see if our respective tools were conforming to a compatible communication model using the chosen CORBA technology. The diagram helped to agree uniformity of interface design and distribution of work.

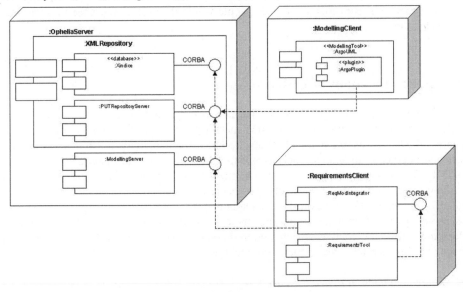

Figure 8.2: Example implementation diagram

Before moving on, look again at the diagram in figure 8.2. This provides an example where a UML tool was inadequate, and the actual diagram was therefore drawn directly in Word. UML modelling tools currently lack the ability to express such composite diagrams where so much detail is shown in implementation diagrams, i.e. in this particular example we are showing deployment units within nodes and showing subcomponents within parent components. This diagram was produced through collaborative effort by circulating a Word document around partners by email. Such exchanges of diagrams were invaluable when face to face meetings were not possible. At times many face to face meetings were required, and this is something that we will be discussing as the next topic within this section.

However, before you carry on with this chapter we suggest that you take some time out to think about the following activity. It is an open activity to encourage you to take some time now to consider your own experiences. There are no solutions to this type of activity as such (alas), but such activities are still helpful and should not be underestimated. Much of the time this can be compared to our modelling activities – we become a little too fixated on whether the answer to the activity or question is *right*. Taking the time to find out what you think or how this relates to your own past experiences is still a valuable exercise.

A: Consider a project you have been involved in (or one that may be coming up) where there was uncertainty or lack of clarity about a technology, and how it would be used. Think, for example, about how you assess the scope of affect it has on the project – how many people and *who* does it affect? Can you see any means by which UML could help you in the future? Think about a series of questions about the particular technology and determine if UML can help address or raise any of these questions. This does not necessarily have to be at a low software communication level, there may be higher level concerns about how people would themselves interface through given technologies.

Informal applications of UML

It is a requirement of EU projects that partners arrange and attend regular face to face meetings (three or four per year). At such meetings we found that the use of UML in a dynamic mode was essential for clarifying technical matters. This mostly involved using class and interaction diagrams. Such uses were often what we call disposable applications of UML. By this we mean that UML was applied to explore ideas during meetings and the resulting diagrams may not find themselves being documented or incorporated into further models. This application tends to be on a small scale, for example to explore parts of the system or parts of models, exploring their structure (class diagrams) and resulting interaction between components (interaction diagrams). The picture in figure 8.3 shows an image of a flip chart taken from one of our technical meetings.

Q: *Study the image in figure 8.3 carefully. What can you distinguish amongst the variety of drawings shown in the flip chart image? Do any key parts of the image stand out as recognisable UML? Take a few moments to consider this before reading on, as this question will be addressed in the following text.*

Amongst the other doodles on the flipchart you might be able to make out a class diagram and sequence diagram. The image shows that in such meetings the drawings themselves can be quite erratic and messy – people are focussed much more on an exchange of ideas than a neat representation of a UML diagram. The point is that the diagrams served a purpose at the time to clarify the way a number of developers were thinking. Having used a basic flipchart we might be presented with the problem of how to store such diagrams. Of course, someone could be made responsible for taking the flipchart page, and/or the model could be redrawn and circulated after the meeting. Technology can also offer us solutions. In the case of the OPHELIA project digital cameras were used to capture and record images for subsequent circulation. Certain of these images may then be turned into more formally recorded models and stored in UML tools. Others may be discarded after a time as they have served their purpose and any form of recording in a UML modelling tool would have been an unnecessary overhead. Other technological solutions may be to use a form of electronic whiteboard i.e. a whiteboard that can automatically transfer data into a UML modelling tool. A number of such technologies now exist, and some references are given at the end of this chapter.

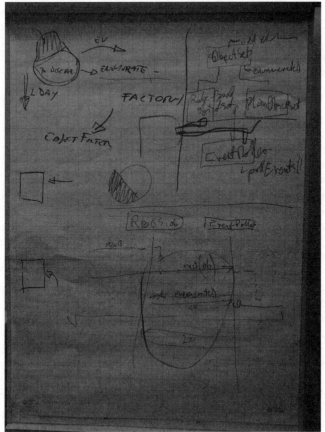

Figure 8.3: Example of dynamic and informal application of UML

A word of caution

It is important to keep in mind the fact that producing and recording a UML diagram in itself is not the end product. There should be a purpose for *creating* a UML diagram in the first place, and a reason for its subsequent *recording* and possible *maintenance*. A diagram should be used to raise questions or/and in turn to answer questions. The UML diagram, in a project such as we have described here, serves a purpose to stimulate interaction between people and force them to engage in discussion.

A: Think about a project that you have experience of. A variety of models, diagrams, documents would no doubt have been produced (UML or otherwise). What was the initial purpose of the project artefact, and did that purpose change over time? Since this activity is based on your own experience there is no single solution. However, connected with this activity there is further discussion of the OPHELIA project on the Web site which accompanies this book.

Irrespective of any agreed methodology it is important to agree a general level of usage of UML. By this we mean to clearly identify the purpose of diagrams being created, and to acknowledge if that purpose changes over time. This will help to identify whether the diagrams should be maintained as part of the ongoing project. For whose benefit are diagrams drawn and maintained? There should always be a purpose.

8.2.2 Scenarios of Usage

A key contribution to the success of many projects is the early identification of scenarios of usage. This was particularly important for the OPHELIA project due to the extra complexities of the distributed project team. We suffered some confusion in our project because we failed to do this to a sufficiently early stage. We took it for granted that we understood the problem that we were all trying to address, because we all know that distributed software development is difficult – don't we? We realised that, as interesting as the series of requirements was, it was not helping the distributed project team focus on the problem with distributed modelling that we were trying to address.

Before we carry on into some illustrations, it is perhaps helpful to discuss a little more about what we mean by a scenario of usage (this may also be referred to as a user scenario). A scenario describes a particular user getting something useful done. Scenarios are typically linked to use case modelling, where a use case is a set of similar scenarios all with the same type of user and all ending when the user finds out that the process is complete. The user must begin a use case and must know when it is complete. The user is an active entity (represented in the use case diagram as an actor) and communicates with the system to achieve the goal of the use case. User scenarios are not just a series of requirements – though we would anticipate that there should ideally be some mapping between user scenarios and the eventual set of requirements.

The identification of scenarios of usage is important to the requirements capture process and to the project as a whole. It's about giving people a focus – especially when people are working in a distributed manner, as in a project such as OPHELIA. It is easy to lose the plot of what we are trying to do once we become embroiled in a range of technical issues, requirements and related discussions.

While it is common to think of user scenarios at the use case level, there is a more abstract level that can really help us find common ground. In her paper, *Ending Requirements Chaos*, Susan August talks about the importance of the *day in the life* system context use case. The view we are taking here mirrors Susan's view that the scenario of usage is a high level usage story that can help us to clarify and evaluate both the problem *and* the solution. A key factor in the OPHELIA project is to achieve an understanding of how people work in distributed software engineering project.

Our example scenario will consider how modellers in particular work, since that relates well with the topic of this book. This scenario applies to any modelling activity, i.e. what the modellers are modelling is not itself a factor, we are concerned with how they go about producing the model. So it could be related to business modelling, software engineering or broader systems engineering.

In this particular example of modelling scenarios of usage we applied the diagrams shown in the following *modelling scenarios of usage* information box.

Modelling Scenarios of Usage	**CLASS DIAGRAM**	clarify units of granularity associated with modelling and related terminology (specifically the meaning and associations between a Project, Model and Diagram).
	USE CASE DIAGRAM	used to show the high level picture, to give the scope of the problem and the key actors involved/affected.
	ACTIVITY DIAGRAM	used to document the actual scenarios of usage.

We have also experimented using interaction diagrams to model scenarios of usage, in particular we have explored the use of sequence diagrams. Our experience is that the activity diagram offers more flexibility, especially allowing clear identification of alternative paths through a number of decision points. A further difficulty with interaction diagrams is the need to identify more explicitly the objects that will interact. These can often be at such an abstract/artificial level that they are not entirely helpful and can confuse people.

The scenario of usage that we are going to present and discuss here concerns our experience working on the modelling module and our understanding of how modellers work. Our work on the OPHELIA project makes use of two different CASE tools; Rational Rose and argoUML. Rational Rose was chosen to document the scenarios of usage work, specifically for its ability to handle activity diagrams well and also Web publish the resulting model. We'll return to the benefits of Web publishing later on.

The class diagram in figure 8.4 was used to clarify terminology used in our project. We found that we were often talking about projects, models and diagrams and it was clear that at times we were all talking about different things. In particular, certain partners viewed a situation where a project would always have a single model file. This view differs from that of certain other partners and the model presented in figure 8.4 reflects a much more flexible view where a project may have one or more associated models. Now you might well be thinking that you follow the thoughts of one or either camp. This in itself is not important, but the fact that the class diagram in figure 8.4 brings these differences out in the open *is important*.

A key factor of concern to the Modelling Module in the proposed OPHELIA environment is that the model provides the level of locking to avoid consistency errors i.e. if a user gains access to a model file, other users would be prohibited from also making changes to that model file. Under such circumstances all other users can have only a read-only version of the same file.

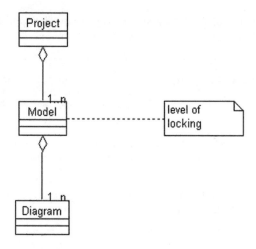

Figure 8.4: Class diagram clarifying terminology

So, having clarified a level of terminology and its usage we moved on to explore a use case diagram. This is focussing on the use of models, the actors who create them, update them and reference them.

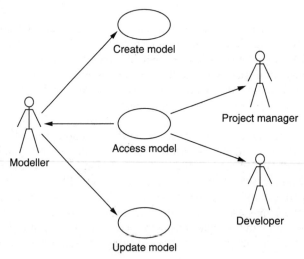

Figure 8.5: Use case diagram use of model in project

Figure 8.5 provides a simple view showing the actor roles of **Modeller**, **Project Manager** and **Developer**. Remember that in use case modelling we can have the same physical person on a project taking on a number of roles – the important thing is to identify the role itself. In this case, the point being made is that the model will only be changed (created or updated) by someone taking on the **Modeller** role. The use cases in figure 8.5 reflect things that the distributed tool environment (in this case OPHELIA) needs to support. Specifically facilitating the storage and retrieval of a model.

The environment itself is not presently supporting the modelling activity itself. For this we will consider the activities associated with modelling and the way in which modellers work. This is illustrated in the activity diagram in figure 8.6.

The point we are making here, and a point for you to consider from your own experience, is that UML modelling tools themselves do not necessarily support the modelling process. Their role is to support the recording and documentation of models. The distinction is quite important. Based on our own experience we would advocate that modelling activities are participatory and at their best when all participants are physically present (as in the informal usage described earlier where a flipchart is used). We would not have dreamt of all sitting around a terminal.

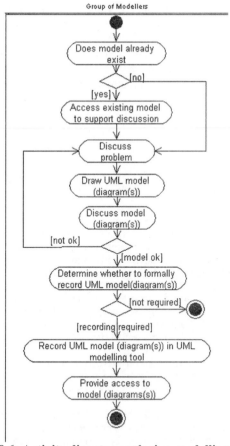

Figure 8.6: Activity diagram exploring modelling activity

A: Think about a project environment that you have worked in, or may be working in at present. What scenarios of usage can you determine? Since this activity is based on your own experience there is, again, no single solution. However, connected with this activity there is further discussion of the OPHELIA project on the Web site which accompanies this book and you will find further scenarios of usage described there.

8.3   Summary and discussion

This case study has covered a range of issues, but they all bring us back to consider what we are trying to achieve in a given application of UML. In particular, what are we trying to communicate and with whom. In thinking about this further, let us now consider some of the practical issues in presenting UML diagrams. Whilst the support offered by UML modelling tools is improving we are still often constrained by the limitations of the tool's graphical capabilities. As an example, consider our previous point about the implementation diagram shown in figure 8.2. At present there are no UML modelling tool's that would allow you to draw the diagram in such a way – they all impose their own limitations. All tools impose their own layout restrictions or particular quirks of presenting a diagram in a certain way, for example in Rational Rose use cases cannot be drawn with text inside them, which when hand drawing diagrams is the most natural approach.

The UML tools can be complex for quick illustrations – which is one reason that most of us would not actually sit at such a tool to develop a model. We prefer to use techniques, such as white boards and flipcharts to support quick drawing and changing of ideas.

The following provides a summary of key points and lessons that we learned through the project described in this case study:

Layout   the physical layout can aid or detract from the diagram's ability to communicate. For example, consider the activity diagram in figure 8.6 where there is a synchronisation bar shown across the **Traceability Module** swimlane. Strictly speaking it is nothing to do with the **Traceability Module** – the synchronisation is between the **Instigator** and **Reactor** swimlanes. We could take the time to rearrange and reorder the swimlanes, but at the same time there is perhaps benefit in seeing this new swimlane placed between the **Instigator** and **Reactor** giving the visual impression of a mediator. The layout of the diagram has to be a compromise at the end of the day.

Level of detail   as with any modelling exercise, it is important to use an appropriate level of detail in the model. Identify what you need to focus on, and don't overwhelm people with unnecessary detail.

Physical size   the resulting physical size of the diagram can become a problem in presenting it to people. For example, consider the difficulties in presenting large diagrams in text documents that are limited to A4, as most documents are. Scroll bars can help when looking at such models on the screen, but this only helps up to a certain diagram size before people find it difficult to see the whole.

Communication
this concerns the physical medium used to present diagrams to other people (for example, other project team members). If you have spent considerable time documenting diagrams in a tool such as Rational Rose, do you really want to spend time then reproducing information in a Word document? It is important to think how you expect to communicate information between people. A recommendation from our experience is to consider the benefits of Web publishing the models as it makes use of material already keyed into a modelling tool. This is particularly beneficial where, as in our example, the people who are communicating the scenarios of usage are all members of the project team and therefore of a comparable technical skill level and familiar with navigating round tools and the Internet. However, with a little more instruction and detailed documentation the technology could also be used to communicate model information with people who are less technically skilled or conversant in UML.

Geographically and culturally separate groups
such project working is always going to be complex. In such projects an element of well placed and carefully crafted UML can help significantly – remember that old adage about a picture can replace a thousand words? In projects where language may be an additional barrier to communication the use of diagrams is even more important.

Different levels of experience with UML
this again concerns the use of an appropriate level of UML and endeavour to keep it simple. Our view is that the resulting scenarios of usage should be kept simple – the diagrams should be fairly intuitive and avoidance of dressing up the notation.

It is also important to accept that there are limitations of using UML. It does not always lend itself to particularly stimulating diagrams, and for this reason there will always be other types of diagrams and images that you will want to use to communicate ideas – especially through publications and promotional material where less formal diagrams are helpful and appropriate.

Whilst our focus here has concerned the added complexity of supporting people who are working in distributed environments, the issues about improving communication really work for any type of project. The following are our top tips that we would recommend for other projects to consider regarding scenarios of usage and application of UML:

Start Early
Start to identify scenarios of usage early in project. There is often still so much focus on technology that the project team may forget what the problem is that they are trying to resolve (especially in a project such as ours).

Key Scenarios
Identify key scenarios of usage rather than trying to identify them all – again information overload does not help to support project team focus.

Iterations and Increments
Continue to base work on iterations. Accept that the appropriate level of detail will be developed through a series of increments and refinements through iterative developments.

Experiment with notation	Experiment early on with notation. Identify the level of UML experience of team, and how this might influence the range and scope of notation that may be appropriate – or additional training that the project members may require
Layout	Be aware of implications of layout of diagrams – extra information may be implied intentionally or otherwise!
Web Publishing	Make use of Web publishing facilities to communicate scenarios of usage (and other model elements)
Compromise	Be aware of compromises made in the model development when addressing clarity of presentation issues i.e. compromises made to keep the diagram streamlined and of an acceptable physical size.

Further reading

The following two articles are particularly helpful in discussing the importance of scenarios of usage:

Catherine Conner and Leonard Callejo, Requirements Management Practices for Developers, Rational Edge, July 2002, http://www.therationaledge.com/content/jul_02/m_requirementsManagement_cc.jsp

Susan August, Ending Requirements Chaos, Rational Edge, August 2002, http://www.therationaledge.com/content/aug_02/m_endingChaos_sa.jsp

The project discussed in this chapter was funded by the OPHELIA (Open Platform and meTHodologies for deVELopment tools and IntegrAtion in a distributed environment) project (IST-2000-28402-2000-20002). Further information about this project can be found through the following resources and publications:

Pauline Wilcox, Michael Smith, Alan Smith, Rob Pooley, Lachlan MacKinnon and Rick Dewar, *OPHELIA: An architecture to facilitate software engineering in a distributed environment*, 15th International Conference on Software and Systems Engineering and their Applications (ICSSEA), December 3–5, Paris, France 2002.

Rick Dewar, Lachlan MacKinnon, Rob Pooley, Alan Smith, Michael Smith and Pauline Wilcox, *The OPHELIA Project: Supporting Software Development in a Distributed Environment*, IADIS WWW/Internet 2002, 13–15 September 2002

Official OPHELIA Project Web site http://dev.omega-sistemi.it/

Heriot-Watt OPHELIA web site http://www.macs.hw.ac.uk/ophelia/

The Web published scenarios of usage (including the Modelling example discussed in this case study and others) can be found at the Web site associated with this book (see Preface for details).

9

Review of Case Studies

In this final chapter of Section Two, we want to take time to review some of the key issues raised in the previous four case study chapters. This provides an opportunity for us to pull together a number of points that we would like to encourage you to think about in your future application of the UML.

In Chapter 1 we mentioned three key questions that people ask us time and time again in connection with learning about the UML. As a reminder these were:

How do I use the UML?	This is a question often asked by people once they have started to get their head around the notation.
What should I do?	People often want to know which diagram to use for which problem.
How can I get a neat solution?	People are often seeking an impractical neat outcome from their UML modelling.

We hope that, having worked your way through the previous four case studies you now see some of the answers to these questions. The first two questions relate to modelling generally (not the UML specifically) – our answer is that it is important that you determine what it is that you are trying to achieve. Once you have done that you can begin to look at the UML and see how it might help you with a given modelling problem. It is much more important to look at what you are trying to do, and then try a range of diagrams to see which of them help you to take a problem forward in a given situation. We hope that through this text we have perhaps freed up your thinking and what you can do with UML. In particular trying to shake of this need for a neat or correct solution. We would argue that any use of any UML diagram that takes a problem further is a good application.

9.1 What did the case studies tell us?

The world is full of a seemingly endless supply of case studies. Our choice of the four in this book aimed to provide you with a range of different scenarios through which to consider the application of UML. The case studies tackled different types of problems, showing the use of UML in a different light.

Importantly, the case studies also considered different levels of detail. The key point being made is that there is not just one level that is appropriate for modelling. In particular we don't need to be down to the nuts and bolts level to achieve something that is useful and appropriate. Certain case studies addressed high level considerations of business operations, for example in the Trusty Car Company case study in Chapter 5. At other times, lower level timing details were considered, as in the Road Junction case study in Chapter 7.

What else do the case studies tell us about the application of UML? Look again at table 9.1 (we say *again* since it was first introduced in Chapter 1). This table is a refresher of the core UML elements and the case studies that they appeared in. Let's consider the implications of this table again and our choice of case studies.

	Trusty Car Company	Playing Games	Road Junction	Supporting Distributed Working
Use Case diagram	✓	✓	✓	✓
Class diagram	✓	✓	✓	✓
Sequence diagram	✓	✓	✓	✓
Collaboration diagram		✓	✓	✓
Deployment diagram		✓		✓
Statechart		✓	✓	
Package diagram				
Activity diagram	✓			✓
Profile for schedulability, performance and time			✓	
Business Modelling	✓			

Table 9.1: UML usage across case studies

You will see that some UML diagrams turn up time and time again across the case studies. Such diagrams are primarily the class, interaction, activity and use case diagram, and perhaps to a lesser extent the state chart.

This is not just typical of the case studies that we have picked, nor necessarily a result of the way that we model. These diagrams can be considered the most generally useful and therefore core diagrams in the UML. We would recommend that these are the diagrams that you should look to first and foremost in tackling a modelling problem, as most often you will find them helpful. That is not to say that other parts of the UML have nothing to offer. We hope that we have given good examples of where other elements are appropriate. For example, package and implementation diagrams as well as some of the developing UML extensions for business modelling and the profile mechanisms (such as the RT profile). We encourage you to look at what these extensions have to offer, but we suggest that many problems can be tackled initially with the core UML.

In particular, we are very aware that some people will regard our failure to use packages as a fundamental mistake. We acknowledge that in reality people use imported packages, create packages for reuse and model management, define subsystems etc. All of these can be supported by package diagrams. In particular, a detailed understanding of RUP is much easier if the package based view of models, sub-models and models defining different views is adopted. We simply felt they would be rather artificial if used in the studies we chose.

Table 9.2 shows a table that focuses on the core UML diagrams as we have talked about them above (they are shown in no particular order). We have also taken the liberty of including the CRC cards. As mentioned earlier in the text, the CRC card technique is not part of the UML. However, since we have personally found this an interesting and relevant supplement to the modelling activity we consider it important to reference it here as earlier in the book. For the purposes of the discussion here we will consider it as one of the available modelling techniques.

		Requirements	Describe / Document Use Cases	System Structure	Elaborate System Structure
Use Case	Static	✓	✓		
Class	Static		✓	✓	✓
Activity	Dynamic		✓		✓
Interaction	Dynamic		✓		✓
State	Dynamic				✓
Implementation	Static				✓
CRC Cards	Dynamic				✓
Package	Static	✓	✓	✓	

Table 9.2: Key applications of UML diagrams

Table 9.2 identifies whether each of the diagrams/techniques relates to the modelling of what we call static or dynamic elements. This is an important and helpful distinction to make – are we modelling *things* or *behaviours*? In the majority of modelling activities it is important to consider a balance of both. Ultimately the model being developed needs to be able to demonstrate support for dynamic processes, either related to a business model or a software/hardware model. There must be a system structure that supports this dynamic behaviour, so both static and dynamic model elements need to be considered somewhere along the way.

So which do you start with? We do not have a particularly strong view on whether you should start by modelling dynamic or static elements. Sometimes it might be more intuitive to take one or other approach. Our view would be that whichever helps you to get started is the best approach. For example, in certain situations a number of candidate classes might shout out at you and seem obvious. In that case beginning with an element of class modelling seems appropriate, being supplemented by the CRC technique or interaction diagrams to test out the model to see if it supports key dynamic behaviours. At other times starting with a dynamic modelling approach might help to determine key classes.

We can have many such discussions about how we should start, or which technique should we lead with. One, which you are possibly already familiar with, concerns whether a modelling activity should start with use case modelling or class modelling. People often ask whether use case modelling is relevant at all. This is possibly because of the perceived simplicity of the notation – how can anything so simple be helpful?

For example, is the use case diagram introduced in the Road Junction case study really necessary? This diagram is included again as figure 9.1 here for ease of reference.

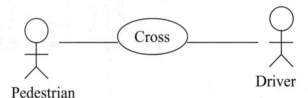

Pedestrian

Driver

Figure 9.1: Use case model of a junction

If a use case diagram has just a single actor and a single use case it can still be helpful. For a start it makes the overall requirement and system interfaces crystal clear. In the above we make clear that the requirement is to support crossing of a junction, and that there are two actors who are involved. This makes a clear statement about the scope of the system – potential or actual. In progressing the model further there might be agreement that only the requirements of the **Pedestrian** are going to be considered in the first instance, but at least the **Driver** actor had to be acknowledged and explicitly removed from the scope as other model elements are developed. We would urge you not to dismiss a diagram because of its perceived simplicity. Conversely, don't think that a model is necessarily good just because it has a set number of use cases, classes etc.

That aside, the other columns in table 9.2 aim to identify categories of problems and which modelling diagram or technique can help us most with that problem. So is this a definitive list? We would suggest not – all such tables can do is give you one view. The point being that if you find that a particular diagram helps you (and your project team) in a given situation then that is the best thing to do.

Through the case studies we have highlighted the benefits of cross-linking between diagrams – showing how the different UML diagrams can be used to elaborate and document a model and how to support cross-checking between diagrams. There are certain key associations between diagrams that we have tried to highlight. These are identified to some extent in table 9.2, but are explicitly shown in the table 9.3 in the following section.

9.2 Outstanding issues

Table 9.3 aims to show a different way of looking at the UML diagrams. Each row in the table represents one of the core UML diagrams (as we identified the *core* diagrams earlier). The columns are titled *can be used to elaborate*. What this table is aiming to show is which diagrams can add further information/clarity to instances of the core diagrams. The term elaboration intentionally encompasses activities such as documentation (which adds further clarity) and model checking.

	CAN BE USED TO ELABORATE							
	Use Case	Class	Activity	Interaction	State	Implementation	CRC Cards	Package
Use Case	✓	✓	✓	✓			✓	✓
Class	✓	✓	✓	✓	✓	✓	✓	✓
Activity			✓					
Interaction			✓	✓				

Table 9.3: Associations between UML diagrams

You will immediately notice a pattern of ticks showing that each core diagram can be elaborated by a diagram of the same type. This makes the point that we have raised in many of the case studies about the use of sub-diagrams of the same type can help to elaborate a primary diagram. What we are saying is that it might be appropriate to further elaborate a high level use case diagram or class diagram in terms of sub-diagrams of the same type. We would argue that this applies to all core UML diagrams.

Other mappings can be made, for example mapping a class to one or more use cases on a use case diagram, or vice versa depending on how the models develop. Helping to look for these possible mappings in your own modelling exercises helps to strengthen the model and also your modelling skills in applying the UML.

There are many applications and connections between diagrams that have not yet been fully explored. You might, for example, like to consider the possibility of taking a sequence diagram and a statechart and combing this information into an activity diagram. What can be expressed this way and what is lost?

One curiosity about the UML concerns the statechart and the activity diagram. Think about these two types of diagrams further. There is a significant cross-over in terms of notation, but there are different applications – but are these real or perceived differences in applications? Look at the ways that we have used activity diagrams and state charts in the case studies. Activity diagrams tend to be used to give a general process view. Statecharts tend to imply a lower level of dynamic modelling, moving towards code and implementation. This is not mandated by the UML – but is perhaps a more natural division of what to use when – or perhaps it is a consequence of our modelling background?

When do you choose to use which variant of interaction diagrams, sequence or collaboration? Quite often this is a personal matter of preference – people often develop a personal liking for one or other views. Since the majority of modelling tools can automatically convert between the sequence and collaboration diagram representations this often does not matter.

9.3   And finally …

Finally, the following are some key tips:

Engage   Modelling is a practical skill that needs to be developed. The best way to learn about applying the UML is by doing – you have to engage in the modelling activity. We have tried to reinforce that with the activities and questions throughout all of the chapters, but mostly through the four case studies.

Process   We've talked about this throughout the text. Each of the case studies has contained a series of hints and tips for modelling particular types of problem. These are not in themselves a substitute for an acknowledged and agreed process. We shall return to consider this further in the third section of the book (see Chapters 10 and 11).

Explore   Modelling is a journey of exploration, and it's about what you learn along the way and using and developing your skills to ensure that you identify and ask appropriate questions. Accept that there is not one single correct answer to a problem. Many solutions may be practical given a range of assumptions.

Granularity   Break away from thinking about a single model or a single view. The case studies showed that sub-diagrams could be helpful in highlighting particular points – you don't need to add more and more information to a single diagram. This is where packages can be particularly important, allowing a group of related diagrams to form a sub-model.

Linking   Explore the links that can be made between diagrams. This helps you to document as well as strengthen the model.

Experiment   Combinations of UML diagrams are possible (though not supported by many modelling tools). Consider, for example, the notion of combining collaboration diagrams within state charts. This is shown in two of our case studies to be a helpful association to make – don't be afraid of experimenting with the notation and diagrams.

Since we've made the point that modelling is such a practical and engaging activity, it seems fitting to end this section with a final activity. Having read through this chapter, you might now like to review the case study chapters again and consider the following activity.

A: In reviewing the case studies ask yourself again what do the diagrams convey to you? Do they give you a way in to understanding a range of problems related to the particular case study (that is not the same as saying do you agree with each of the diagrams). What questions do the diagrams make you ask? In what ways are they better (or at times worse) than a page and a half of text-based description?

Part Three

Assessing and Evaluating Process Maturity

10

The Capability Maturity Model for Software

The importance of process has been emphasised at many points throughout the previous sections of this book. This was most notable in the case studies in Part Two where we repeatedly made the point that there is no single process that will suit in all situations. This, we feel, is a mistake that many organisations continue to make. The answer is not just to pick on any single methodology and apply it to the letter. It is important to give thought to the choice of methodology to adopt, and ensure that it is applied to the situation in hand in an appropriate manner.

Each new methodology and technology comes with its own set of promises about the gains an organisation can make in productivity and quality by its particular adoption. Each can often appear to make promises such that it appears to be the solution to all of the organisation's problems. Many of these promises remain unrealised as organisations have a basic inability to manage process, in particular the software process. If an organisation is fundamentally undisciplined and chaotic then there is no methodology in the world that will make everything better, in itself.

There are a number of standards that attempt to certify the management of organisations. For example, ISO9001 and TickIT have been widely used within the UK. In this chapter we introduce the Capability Maturity Model (CMM) for Software as an alternative vehicle to assess an organisation's abilities. This includes an introduction of the CMM in the wider sense, and, specifically, the CMM for Software.

There is general agreement on the need for methods and processes to support problem solving. The agreement identifies a need to solve the problem in hand, but also to demonstrate control and improvement of the processes themselves. The CMM, as its name suggests, is about the *capability* and *maturity* of an organisation. It is a model that identifies the requirements that a process needs to satisfy to improve in both capability and maturity. The CMM model provides organisations with guidance on how they can gain control of processes and evolve through a number of incremental stages towards a culture of software engineering and management excellence. Thus, it guides software organisations in selecting process improvement strategies, helping them to determine their current maturity and undertake practical activities that encourage this to improve steadily.

Does this perhaps all sound too good to be true? Well, only time will tell, but the CMM appears to be offering a wealth of practical advice, which is refreshing in itself. In working through this chapter you will learn more about what the CMM is (and also therefore what it is not – for it is, in itself, certainly no silver bullet for all of your organisation's problems) and also how important it has become for organisations thus far in its relatively short life.

10.1 Background to CMM

The CMM for Software was developed and promoted through the Software Engineering Institute (SEI) at Carnegie Mellon University. The framework is based on extensive research work carried out by the SEI and the MITRE Corporation, establishing and monitoring maturity levels in software engineering organisations since the mid 1980s. The CMM for Software was initially released as version 1.0 in the early 1990s. Following feedback from software organisations and individual professionals, the current version of the CMM for Software (v1.1) was released. This is the version that will be referred to in the remainder of this chapter.

Other standards and frameworks exist that support audit and/or certification processes, and these can be viewed as competitors with the CMM. For example, you may have experience yourself with industry standards such as ISO9000/9001 or TickIT. Alternatively, you may have experience with the internal standard promoted by an organisation.

The CMM framework can be used in a number of ways:

Seeking certification	this is the most formal application of the framework and would involve an organisation actively seeking to establish its maturity level against this framework.
Internal review	an organisation may undertake an internal review of its current practices and processes with reference to the framework. This is a less formal application, though it may well be a precursor to seeking official certification as described above.
Tool/methodology comparison	the framework identifies key criteria required to support mature processes. As part of that, a company will most likely be selecting tools and methodologies to support those practices. Making such choices is often difficult, as it requires an identification of a common basis for comparison (assuming that an organisation is sufficiently mature to avoid basing the choice on anything other than price alone). The CMM makes an ideal framework for comparing tools and methodologies.

We'll be returning to explore the third application above in detail in Chapter 11. For now let us move on to consider what the CMM actually looks like in more detail. The initial way of looking at the CMM is to view it as comprising five maturity levels. These are the levels that organisations can align themselves with. Each maturity level is a well-defined, evolutionary plateau toward achieving a mature software process. These five levels are numbered and named in the diagram in figure 10.1.

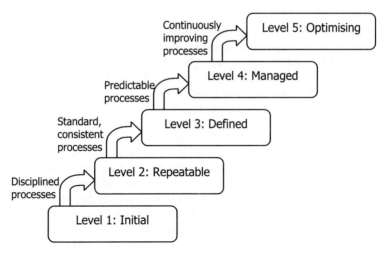

Figure 10.1: The five levels of CMM for software

Figure 10.1 shows the starting point for all organisations at the bottom of the diagram. The starting point is referred to numerically as level 1, or in descriptive terms as the *Initial* level. This level involves a fair amount of chaos and fire fighting; things we have no doubt all experienced.

From here the only way is up (so the CMM would suggest). Each subsequent level is an incremental improvement in an organisation's abilities to implement and manage processes. There are, necessarily, improvements that an organisation needs to make in order to move to the next level. For example, in moving from level 1 to level 2 an organisation needs to demonstrate that it supports a set of disciplined processes. If it can demonstrate that, then it reaches level 2. This would, as the name suggests, infer that the organisation has *Repeatable* behaviour. Repeatable behaviour implies an element of control has been established. Each level adds more refined levels of control and process management, until the highest level is achieved.

At this point the organisation demonstrates that it is in the position to optimise its approaches through a continual process improvement schedule. Each level builds on the previous level achieved, so there is a cumulative benefit in moving up through the levels. Note that the diagram implies relationships and progression between successive levels only – there is no offered scope to leapfrog past levels.

This gives you an outline view of the CMM, its levels and the associations between levels. There is obviously more to it than that as we will go on to review. Before doing so, why not consider the following interesting UML exercise (just in case you thought we'd left that behind).

Q: *Look at the diagram in figure 10.1. How could this be drawn using UML? You might think that this is a strange thing to consider, but given what we have talked about in previous chapters, UML is just a graphical notation and can be used in drawing many diagrams. What about representing the same information from figure 10.1 using a class or activity diagram? What is gained or lost in doing so? An example solution will be presented in the text as you read on.*

As an example solution to the above activity, consider the class diagram in figure 10.2. This shows the levels as a conceptual class, with each subsequent level inheriting from the previous one. That is quite a nice way of thinking about the characteristics of the organisation in moving between successive levels. We've lost the visual cue from figure 10.1 where each level is drawn physically on top of the previous implying the foundational view of the CMM (though you could draw the class diagram the other way up!). The point about using UML to draw such a diagram is an interesting one though, and aims to get you thinking about applying UML in places where you may not have otherwise seen it fit.

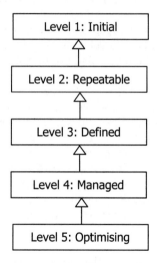

Figure 10.2: The five levels of CMM for software (UML'd)

Let us now look in more detail at each of the five levels, and the maturity characteristics of an organisation that are present at each level. An outline description is provided in the following:

1. Initial   The software process at this level is generally undefined. Work is chaotic and reactionary. The success or failure of projects is down to the effort of individuals who seem to be able to pull things together at the end of the day.

2. Repeatable   Basic project management processes are established to track cost, schedule and functionality. The necessary process discipline is in place to repeat earlier successes in projects with similar applications.

3. Defined   The software process for management and development activities is documented, standardised and integrated into a standard software process for the organisation. All projects use an approved, tailored version of the process.

4. Managed   Detailed metrics of the software process and product quality are collected. Both the software process and products are quantitatively understood and controlled.

5. Optimised   Continuous process improvement is enabled by quantitative feedback from software process and from piloting innovative ideas and technologies.

10.2 The importance of maturity

The previous section has provided us with a basic introduction to the CMM. It is necessary at this point to consider the meaning and importance of maturity. In a general sense, when we talk about maturity we talk about things becoming older and wiser – a key point being that there is evidence of learning through experience. This also relates to the concept of an organisation's maturity.

Chapter 4 discussed the need for a methodology or software process. While there are many variants of process models, there is general agreement in these on the need to start with an accepted set of requirements. It is just as important now that we establish the requirements of a methodology that we are going to use, so that we can determine its appropriateness. This is where the CMM for Software can help. The CMM for Software is defined and described in the following section. We will see this framework applied in Chapter 11 where we will use it as the basis to compare a number of methodologies.

Each maturity level indicates a level of process capability. In moving from level 1 to level 2 the process capability has been elevated from ad-hoc to disciplined by introducing sound project management controls. So how is that achieved? We'll dig a little further into the CMM by looking at its structure. This is illustrated in figure 10.3.

Each *maturity level* contains a number of *key process areas* (KPA). Each KPA has a series of associated activities which, when performed together, achieve a set of *goals*. All goals of a KPA must be achieved to satisfy that KPA and therefore achieve a certain level of maturity in the model.

The KPAs are organised by *common features*. These are attributes that address whether the implementation and institutionalisation of a KPA is effective, repeatable and lasting. There are five defined common features as follows:

Commitment to perform   Describes the actions the organisation must perform to ensure that the process is established and will endure. It requires establishing policies and securing support from senior management.

Ability to perform   Describes preconditions that need to exist in the project/organisation to implement the identified processes competently. Typically requires allocation of resources, organisational structures and training.

Activities performed   Describes roles and procedures required to implement a KPA. Activities typically involve establishing plans, procedures, performing and tracking work and taking corrective actions.

Measurement and Analysis   Describes the need to measure the process and measure performance. This feature would define the means to take such measurements.

Verifying implementation   Describes the steps to ensure the activities are performed in compliance with the defined process. This will typically involve reviews, audits by management and software quality audits.

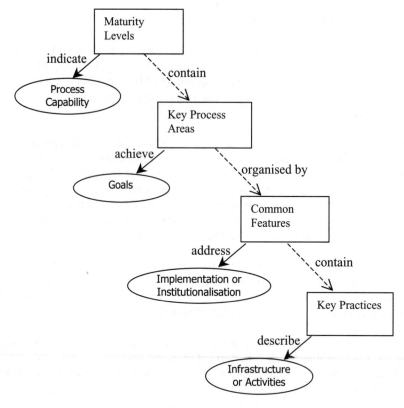

Figure 10.3: The CMM structure

The common features are characterised by a number of *key practices*. These are most typically expressed as a written description of *what* is do be done within a particular organisation to satisfy the goals of the KPA.

A more detailed breakdown of the KPAs is helpful in understanding the CMM further, and will be a key to our use of the CMM to compare methodologies in the next chapter. The diagram in figure 10.1 illustrated the five maturity levels defined in the CMM for Software. Each of these levels is a progression to achieving a mature software process. According to the CMM, in order to achieve a specific maturity level an organisation must satisfy (and be able to demonstrate) the relevant key process areas (KPAs). The KPAs are shown in figure 10.4 against the respective maturity level.

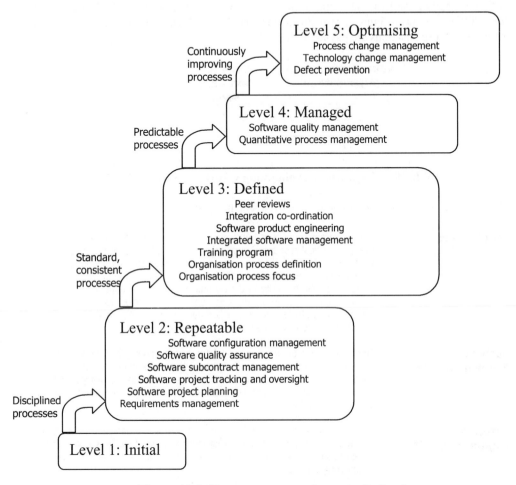

Figure 10.4: Key process areas by maturity level

Note that the KPAs are shown in a particular order and manner in figure 10.4. The implication is that there is an appropriate and recommended order in which the KPAs be addressed, with each KPA acting as a suitable and necessary foundation in order to consider the next KPA. For example, in looking at level 2 of the model, the first KPA is shown to be *Requirements Management*. This seems a logical place to begin, but more than that the diagram shows this to be a foundation KPA in order to address the next which is *Software Project Planning*.

10.3 Current status

The CMM is sponsored by the United States Department of Defense (DoD) and has already been adopted by many organisations worldwide in order to improve the way that they develop software. The gathering momentum can be checked out via the Carnegie Mellon Software Engineering Institute Web site (http://seir.sei.cmu.edu/pml/index.asp last accessed June 2003). Summary figures are included in table 10.1, which give an indication of the attention that organisations are paying to the CMM.

Approx. number of organisations	CMM for Software level
100+	5
80+	4
110+	3
50+	2

Table 10.1: Organisations obtaining CMM for software levels

The CMM is also spreading into other areas of specialism, for example:

People CMM
This is a framework that helps organisations to address issues relating to the most critical resource i.e. people. It is based on current best practices in fields such as human resources, knowledge management, and organisational development. The People CMM helps organisations to characterise the maturity of their workforce practices, establish a program of continuous workforce development, set priorities for improvement actions, integrate workforce development with process improvement, and establish a culture of excellence.

Software Acquisition CMM
This framework provides a model for benchmarking and improving the software acquisition process. It follows the same architecture as the CMM for Software, but with a unique emphasis on acquisition issues and the needs of individuals and groups who are planning and managing software acquisition efforts

Systems Engineering CMM
This describes the essential elements of an organisation's systems engineering process that must exist to ensure good systems engineering. In addition, it provides a reference for comparing actual systems engineering practices.

Integrated Product Development CMM
Provides an integrated product development (IPD) framework to guide organisations in IPD design, development, appraisal, and improvement. The resulting model outlines a systematic approach to product development that achieves a timely collaboration of necessary disciplines throughout the product life cycle to better satisfy customer needs. It typically involves a teaming of the functional disciplines to integrate and concurrently apply all necessary processes to produce an effective and efficient product that satisfies the customer's needs

In addition to the above CMM work programs, Carnegie Mellon are also progressing work concerning Capability Maturity Model Integration (CMMI).

Further reading

The following is an excellent reference for the CMM, and it has the added advantage of being available via the Internet (for free!).

> Paulk, M.C., Curtis, B., Chrissis, M. and Weber, C.V. (1993a), *Capability Maturity Model for Software (Ver 1.1)*, Technical Report CMU/SEI-93-TR-24, Software Engineering Institute, Pittsburgh. http://citeseer.nj.nec.com/303578.html [last accessed June 2003]

In addition the following two textbooks elaborate on the practical nature of the CMM, the latter is interesting as it shows an alternative version of the framework that concerns people processes rather than software.

> Jalote P., *CMM in Practice: Processes for Executing Software Projects at Infosys*, Addison-Wesley, ISBN 0201616262

> Curtis, W., Hefley, W.E. and Miller, S.A., *The People Capability Maturity Model: Guidelines for Improving the Workforce*, Addison-Wesley, ISBN 0210604450

Finally, for an update on current developments and specific information on CMM initiatives you can consult the Carnegie Mellon Software Engineering Institute CMM Web site http://www.sei.cmu.edu/cmm/cmms/cmms.html

11

Evaluating Process Models

The importance of applying an appropriate process or methodology has been discussed previously in this book at various points, but most notably in Chapter 4. There is also general agreement on this within the IT profession. That said, ask yourself how much time is devoted to the pursuit of choosing and evaluating a given methodology? What are the criteria by which a given process model is adopted by an organisation, or the criteria by which an organisation will develop its own? This is the subject of this chapter. Our aim here is to show how the CMM for Software can be used as a framework to explore, compare and evaluate the suitability of methodologies. We are not, however, trying to infer that the CMM is the answer to all of our problems in choosing a methodology. It does, however, at least provide one such mechanism for making a comparison and therefore evaluation.

We are going to look at three methodologies using the CMM framework introduced in Chapter 10. Are we suggesting three to be a magic number? Well, not really. Exploring one methodology by itself is not too enlightening, as there is nothing to compare it with. That problem is immediately addressed by evaluating two, but adding a third makes for a more interesting and fruitful exercise.

It is also appropriate to consider our choice of which three methodologies to compare. It seems inevitable that we would consider the Rational Unified Process (RUP) as one of our choices. It is making headlines as the methodology of choice for UML practitioners to adopt because (other considerations apart) the RUP comes from the same stable as the UML itself. We consider Catalysis and XP as our other two methodologies. These are three quite different process models, and it is interesting to see just how different such models can be.

A by-product of this chapter is that we may introduce you to a methodology that you have not previously encountered. We briefly mentioned each of these three (RUP, Catalysis and XP) in Chapter 4, but only within an outline introduction to a broad range of different process models. In this chapter we necessarily go into further detail about each in order to have a meaningful comparison.

KEY POINTS	1. To introduce the notion of the CMM for Software as a framework to compare methodologies
	2. To introduce a range of methodologies which you may not previously have considered

It seems fair to point out at the outset that we have no biased opinion regarding any of the three methodologies that we are going to consider. We consider that each has its own merits when applied to an appropriate project.

It is important to remember that the UML itself is a tool/technique, and as such can be applied successfully in a range of different methodologies – not just the ones that advocate the application of UML specifically, such as the RUP. It is important that, as a profession, we move away from such blinkered thinking. You could, for example, successfully apply the RUP using a notation other than UML. The point is that there should be a conscious and informed decision as to *what* you are applying and *why*.

Just in case you had begun to think that the reader participation was complete at this stage in the book, think again. We also include an activity at end of the *Summary and discussion* section of this chapter that encourages you to attempt your own mapping of one or more methodologies using the approach outlined in this chapter.

11.1 Overview of chosen processes

Before we can carry on to make a comparative evaluation of the three methodologies it is important to provide some level of introduction to each of the three. This is not meant to be a detailed description of all that you need to know about each, because we could not possibly have the space for such a detailed treatment of them here. However, we wanted to provide an outline description in the event that one or more are unfamiliar to you. We therefore discuss their origins and key concepts. Further references are provided in the *Further reading* section of this chapter if you would like to find out more.

11.1.1 Rational Unified Process

The RUP is a product of the Rational Corporation. This is the same organisation behind the formation of the UML itself, as discussed in Chapter 3. The RUP is also often referred to as the Unified Process (UP), which sits better alongside the naming of the UML (however, UP is exactly the same methodology as RUP in case you were confused). The RUP has been developed with a significant input from the Objectory Process, which was one of a number of products acquired when Ivar Jacobson's Objectory organisation merged with Rational. The initial acknowledged release of this methodology took place in 1998.

The RUP is most typically, and clearly, described through the diagram shown in figure 11.1 (taken from RUP tool suite documentation). The diagram illustrates a clear structure formed of four serial phases and nine core workflows. The phases map well to the stages of a typical software engineering project, while the workflows relate more to the activities that will be undertaken.

The *Inception* phase concerns the scope and requirements definition of the project, identifying and clarifying the business case for the proposed system. Key tasks during this phase are identified in the workflows, so for the inception phases these include business modelling and requirements engineering, as well as tool selection and process tailoring which are defined within the environment workflow. A key outcome of this phase will be the identification of material to support the go/no-go status of the project.

The *Elaboration* phase concerns the analysis and design workflow, leading to a defined architecture solution to the problem.

The *Construction* phase concerns the detailed design, implementation and testing activities that move towards realising a working solution.

The final *Transition* phase concerns the installation and deployment of the solution at the customer site. The implication in the associated phase and workflows is that the transition is to be managed, with staged delivery and roll out through the organisation. This may involve structured releases of software, from beta through to final.

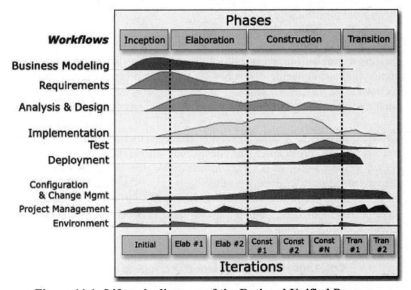

Figure 11.1: Lifecycle diagram of the Rational Unified Process

Note that a key feature of the RUP process is a clear identification of a number of iterations within phases (though the actual number may vary from project to project). This implies a managed approach to work through the identification of milestones and intermediate deliverables to check project progress and early identification of issues and misunderstandings.

Rational offer a full product suite, which aims to assist in the implementation and management of all phases and workflows. A key difficulty in learning about the RUP is that it appears so large, and perhaps verbose. People are often put off by the RUP in the belief that it is a sledgehammer of a methodology to crack a nut of a project. We will return to discuss tailoring of methodologies later in this chapter. The following *Summary of RUP* information box provides a reminder of key characteristics of this process model.

Summary of RUP Characteristics	• Based on sound software engineering principles; requirements driven, iterative progress and review, architecture based • Process driven methodology • Clear structure through phases and workflows • High degree of tool support (through Rational)

11.1.2 Catalysis

The founders of Catalysis are Desmond D'Souza and Alan Wills. Like many methodologies of any weight, it is based on the combined experiences of IT professionals across a range of projects in different domains, adapting and borrowing much from other methods.

There is no single picture that illustrates the overall Catalysis philosophy. This is perhaps a problem in trying to gain an overall feel for it, certainly at the outset. A common recurring theme in this book is that people benefit greatly from diagrams and pictures to help explain concepts – it lies at the very heart of modelling. So not having such a picture giving an overview of Catalysis is certainly a disadvantage.

Catalysis advocates a tailoring of the concepts to suit the problem at hand. In the introduction to this chapter, we considered whether three was a magic number with regard to the number of our chosen methodologies. Well, there is a recurring theme here since the number three lies at the heart of the Catalysis methodology being based on *three constructs, three levels of modelling* and *three defining principles*. These are summarised in the diagrams in figures 11.2, 11.3 and 11.4 (diagrams adapted from Catalysis documentation).

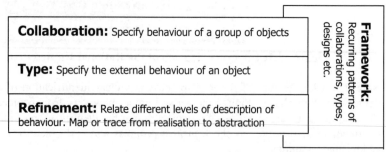

Figure 11.2: Three constructs plus framework

The three constructs in figure 11.2 indicate that *components, types* and *refinement* are key to the Catalysis approach. Interlinking these three is the notion of the *framework*. This maps to the concept of patterns where we set out to relate current modelling and design projects to what has gone before, learning from past experience. The Catalysis method specifies a number of such frameworks (or patterns) for each stage of the development lifecycle – though ideally, through the organisation's maturity, it will learn from its own exercises and develop a family of solutions.

The diagram in figure 11.3 represents the three levels of modelling proposed by Catalysis. These begin with the domain (or business model), leading into modelling at the system level, which in turn follows into the internal modelling. Each level of model adds an increasing level of detail moving through to a system solution/implementation. These levels of modelling aim to separate out and clarify areas of concern. This provides a clear conceptual separation between decisions of *what, who* and *how.*

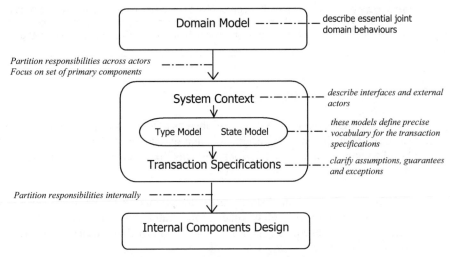

Figure 11.3: Three levels of modelling

The final trio is represented in figure 11.4. The three principles of Catalysis are abstraction, precision and pluggable parts. These principles provide a focus for each level of modelling, influencing the design in a way that fits with the component and pattern based approach that underpins the Catalysis approach.

Principle		Intent
Abstraction	• •	Focus on **essential aspects,** deferring others Create **uncluttered description** of requirements and architecture
Precision	• •	**Expose gaps** and inconsistencies early Make **abstract models accurate,** not fuzzy
Pluggable parts	• •	All work done by **adapting** and **composing** parts Models, architectures and designs are assets

Figure 11.4: Three principles of Catalysis

It is expected that an organisation following the Catalysis approach will adopt an appropriate process model supporting the Catalysis philosophy. This automatically leads to a tailoring of the process, building in necessary project management threads and other characteristics demanded by the particular project. As with many other process models, iteration is a key strength of the Catalysis approach, although the number of such iterations can only be determined on a project by project basis. The following *Summary of Catalysis* information box provides a reminder of key characteristics of this process model.

Summary of Catalysis	• Components and collaboration between them • Application and identification of patterns • Identification of objects and actions (with pre and post conditions) • Recursive, gradual refinement of software, models and designs • More of a philosophy than a rigorous and structured method

11.1.3 Extreme Programming

Extreme programming (or XP) is described as a deliberate and disciplined approach to software development. The originators and ongoing custodians of XP are Kent Beck, Ward Cunningham and Ron Jeffries (perhaps there really is something in the number three after all?).

XP has existed as an established process model since 1996/97. It has been proven by application at cost conscious finance and automotive companies like Bayerische Landesbank, Credit Swiss Life, First Union National Bank, DaimlerChrysler and Ford Motor Company.

This process model has enabled a re-examination of software development practices that have become standard operating procedures in many IT organisations and software houses. It is one of several new lightweight software methodologies created to reduce the cost of software. A heavyweight methodology has many rules, practices, and documents (SSADM and RUP fall more into this category). These require discipline and time to follow correctly. A lightweight methodology has only a few rules and practices or ones that are, in principle, easy to follow. The rules and practices of XP can be categorised under the headings of *planning, coding, designing* and *testing*. These are summarised in figure 11.5.

Many of these are self explanatory, while others perhaps need a little more explanation. Key examples are *project velocity* and *spike solution*. The project velocity (or velocity) is a measure of how much work is being done on the project. It is measured by adding up the estimates of the user stories that were finished during the current iteration. It is also important to total up the estimates for the tasks finished during the iteration. Both of these measurements are used for iteration planning. A spike solution is a very simple program to explore potential solutions (basically a prototype). It is merely aimed to test an idea or principle and is in itself likely to be a disposable unit of code.

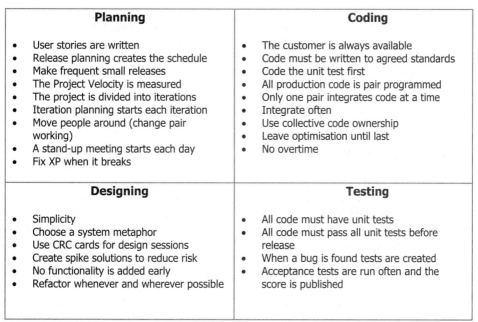

Planning	Coding
• User stories are written • Release planning creates the schedule • Make frequent small releases • The Project Velocity is measured • The project is divided into iterations • Iteration planning starts each iteration • Move people around (change pair working) • A stand-up meeting starts each day • Fix XP when it breaks	• The customer is always available • Code must be written to agreed standards • Code the unit test first • All production code is pair programmed • Only one pair integrates code at a time • Integrate often • Use collective code ownership • Leave optimisation until last • No overtime
Designing	**Testing**
• Simplicity • Choose a system metaphor • Use CRC cards for design sessions • Create spike solutions to reduce risk • No functionality is added early • Refactor whenever and wherever possible	• All code must have unit tests • All code must pass all unit tests before release • When a bug is found tests are created • Acceptance tests are run often and the score is published

Figure 11.5: Simple rules and practices of XP

Frequent iteration and continual, early testing are key features of the XP approach. This can be seen in the diagram in figure 11.6, which shows a typical project structure using XP.

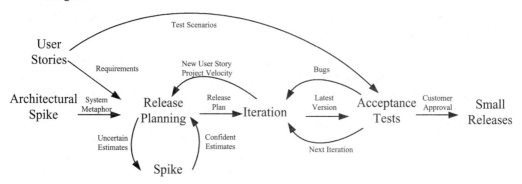

Figure 11.6: Overview of an XP project

The XP approach relies heavily on direct contact between software developers. This either requires that they co-locate (ideal option) or that they share some development environment that would support such working.

The following *Summary of XP* information box provides a reminder of key characteristics of this process model.

Summary of XP	• Specifically oriented towards software development activities • Quick and short iteration cycle • Driven by identification of test scenarios • Heavy emphasis on collaborative (pair) working of software developers • Regarded as one of a number of light or agile processes

11.2 Comparison

In this section we are going to examine together the three process models introduced separately in the previous section. In making any comparison or evaluation we need to identify key characteristics that will be applied equally to each element that we are attempting to assess. In this case, we need to identify measures of comparison for the chosen process models. Our suggestion is that since the CMM defines desirable requirements to support maturity of an organisation's software development process, that the same criteria be used to assess the methodologies.

In this case, this means looking at each of the Key Process Areas (KPAs) of the CMM and looking how each of the process models supports that KPA. This enables a comparison of approaches and also allows us to see which of them may be stronger or weaker in moving to fulfil the KPAs of maturity levels. The comparison is provided through a series of tables in figures 11.7 through 11.10. Each table addresses the KPA associated with achieving a given level of the CMM, from level 2 through to level 5 (we assume that everyone starts out from the initial level 1). A column is then provided for each of the three process models outlined in the previous section with key criteria for mapping against each KPA. The KPA are listed alphabetically within each table.

We begin our discussion by looking at how each of the process models supports level two KPAs. Remember that this level of the CMM is about an organisation demonstrating *repeatable* behaviour. In supporting this we need to look at each of the process models and look to their control and management processes, and any key mechanisms that they employ. This is a key area of each of the process models, although, as figure 11.7 shows, each may appear to tackle this subject at a different level. Of the three process models examined, Catalysis is the one that is most difficult to map to the KPA. This is mostly because the process model is less structured in its definition, and many of the anticipated project management and project support functions are tailored to a particular instance of its application. However, we can begin to see areas of Catalysis where we would look to support the level two KPAs.

Level three of the CMM concerns an organisation establishing a *defined* management and software process. The software process for management and development activities is documented, standardised and integrated into a standard software process for the organisation. All projects use an approved version of the process, which may be tailored to the organisation or project. The mapping of the process models to level three KPA is shown in figure 11.8.

	Key Process Areas	RUP	Catalysis	XP
Level 2	Requirements Management	• Requirements • Config & Chge Mgmt	• Domain model	• User stories • Acceptance Testing
	Software Configuration Management	• Config & Chge Mgmt	• Internal Component Design	• Release Planning • Spike Solutions
	Software Project Checking and Oversight	• Project Mgmnt	• Domain model (checking and review on iteration)	• Release Planning
	Software Project Planning	• Project Mgmnt	• Domain model (partitioning)	• Release Planning
	Software Quality Assurance	• Test • Project Mgmnt	• Iterative development	• Acceptance Testing • Iterations
	Software Subcontract Management	• Project Mgmt	• Project management through partition of domain model	• Release Planning

Figure 11.7 Level Two

	Key Process Areas	RUP	Catalysis	XP
Level 3	Integrated Software Management	• Environment • Project Mgmt	• Component approach • Framework app	• Coding Strategy • Release Planning
	Inter-group Coordination	• Project Mgmt	• Iterations • Component design • Framework app	• Standup Meeting • Pair Coding
	Organisation Process Definition	• Environment	• Defined through project management • Framework review	• Planning rules
	Organisation Process Focus	• Environment • Phase assessments	• Project management • Framework app	• Planning Rules • iterations • Phase Planning • System Metaphor
	Peer Reviews	• Business Modelling • Requirements • Analysis and Design • Implementation • Test	• Iterations	• Pair programming • Iterations • Standup Meeting • Acceptance Tests
	Software Product Engineering	• Analysis and Design • Implementation	• Internal component design • Frameworks	• Pair Programming • Design Rules
	Training Program	• Project Mgmt	• Project management	• Phase Planning

Figure 11.8 Level Three

Level four of the CMM concerns an organisation demonstrating a managed approach, expecting that detailed metrics of the software process and product quality will be collected. Both the software process and products are quantitatively understood and controlled. This is not something that is entirely obvious in the three process models that we are examining here. It is, however, something that each of them *could* support, and if your organisation were aiming to achieve or maintain CMM level 4 then you would be looking to ensure that be supported through the chosen process model. The collation of metrics is supportable by each of the three, and it is again a matter of looking at their structure and establishing where the responsibility for these KPAs most naturally lies.

	Key Process Areas	RUP	Catalysis	XP
Level 4	Quantitative Process Management	• Project Mgmt • End of phase assessments	• Domain model • Framework review/management	• Phase Planning • Planning Rules
	Software Quality Management	• Project Mgmt	• Iterative development	• Iterations • Release Planning • Acceptance Testing

Figure 11.9 Level Four

Finally, level five of the CMM concerns an organisation achieving and maintaining an *optimised* state. This requires that the process model supports continuous process improvement, enabling quantitative feedback from the software process and from piloting innovative ideas and technologies. Although there are ways in which each of the three process methods may support these KPAs, it appears that XP is most rigorous in this area, since striving to support defect prevention and software development maturity are at its core.

	Key Process Areas	RUP	Catalysis	XP
Level 5	Defect Prevention	• Test • Implementation	• Framework application/review • Iterations	• Test scenarios
	Process Change Management	• Environment	• Framework review/management	• Release Planning • User stories
	Technology Change Management	• Elaboration • Analysis and Design	• Framework review	• Spike solution • Release Planning

Figure 11.10 Level Five

Our approach in figures 11.7 through 11.11 was to take a fairly high level view. In the case of the RUP, the associated workflow is identified (see figure 11.1). In the case of Catalysis, the references are mostly to elements of the domain model (see figure 11.3). In evaluating XP, references are made to both the rules and practices (figure 11.5) and project overview diagram (figure 11.6). It would be possible to go down into much more detail in comparing each of the process models, but the more detail you add the more complex the exercise becomes (and is not necessarily better for it). If you have particular experiences with one or more of these process models, then you might have determined alternative/additional points that you might highlight against KPAs. We would be happy to hear from you on this subject, as this is an area of ongoing learning for all of us.

Comparing process models is not an easy activity; nor did we ever pretend that it was going to be. Mostly this is because we are not comparing like with like. You might think that is obvious, but our experience is that people do not take much time out to consider what each process or methodology really has to offer – and as a result people to tend to see them all as pretty much the same.

Some process models have a much more defined and clear structure, such as the RUP, and others do not, such as Catalysis and XP. It is certainly true that the more structured process models are easier to analyse in an exercise such as this. This does not mean, however, that undertaking an exercise such as the one carried out in this section is not worth doing with process models that are a little fuzzier. The key benefit is that it forces you to consider what you understand about each process model, and to look for the area in which a given KPA would be satisfied or addressed. Doing so within the CMM framework gives added confidence in the reason why a process model is being chosen, i.e. for the overall benefit and improving the quality of work carried out by an organisation.

It is important to accept that, depending on their core purpose, certain process models may be stronger in certain areas than others. It might not be immediately obvious where you look within a given process model to satisfy a particular KPA. That tells you something quite important about the process model itself. Of the three process models considered here, we would argue that Catalysis is the hardest to map against the CMM framework. This is mostly due to it being more of a general philosophy for software production as we described in the previous section.

Obviously if you have existing experience of applying a particular process model then you would bring that added value to an exercise such as this. This does not automatically mean that a given process model should be abandoned or dropped. It might be the case that a process model can be adapted and tailored to your own circumstances. Also remember that it may be appropriate to combine one or more methodologies. For example, an organisation could be following the RUP (or a variant of the RUP), while at a more local level following the software development practices advocated by XP. These are not necessarily mutually exclusive.

11.3 Summary and discussion

The CMM for Software provides us with a framework to compare and evaluate methodologies. This is still necessarily a subjective exercise, and as you have seen with the exercise in the previous section, it still is not necessarily easy. The point to realise is that we cannot assume that in comparing processes or methodologies that we are comparing like with like. It is not, regrettably, quite as simple as plugging in comparative values and cranking the handle to determine your ideal methodology. There is still more work in it than that. However, using an established framework such as the CMM for Software, is a step forward to making an informed choice. There will always be additional criteria that you would like to consider, and these could perhaps be supplemented to the approach outlined in the previous section.

We would advocate that it is always the case that a methodology should be tailored to the particular project and organization as appropriate – never take the methodology at face value and apply it verbatim. This is increasingly recognised by those promoting methodologies. As an example, RUP version 2002 provides new support for customising and configuring RUP. From Rational's perspective, the RUP is very much intertwined with their tool support package. The customisation/configuration is delivered through a Plug-In kit for developers and a new tool, RUP Builder. Catalysis is so flexible from the outset, that the very act of applying the process means that you necessarily have to tailor it to your own project, environment and circumstances. Adapting and refining (or at times fixing) XP is automatically accepted as part of the process, as it is identified as a key practice under the Planning category (see figure 11.6). For a good example of a suggested adaptation to the RUP we would recommend checking out the article by Scott Ambler in the *Further reading* section of this chapter.

The application of the CMM framework outlined here also provides a suggested means to learn about new methodologies. Part of the difficulty in learning a new methodology is identifying clearly what it has to offer. You can certainly read all published material concerning a methodology, speak to practitioners and attempt to apply it yourself. Often what is missing, and what makes learning a new methodology difficult is the lack of a reference framework – you are not comparing like for like, which makes the activity difficult. If you have an understanding of the approach outlined in this chapter, then this framework could be used to learn and evaluate a new methodology. You could therefore approach researching a new methodology by looking for how it would support the key process areas outlined in a manner similar to that outlined in the previous section.

A: At this point we would encourage you to look at exploring a further methodology and mapping it into the CMM framework in the manner shown in this chapter. This might consider a methodology that you already know about, or you might consider it an opportunity to learn about a further methodology. Examples to consider are the OPEN process, the Object-Oriented Software Process (OOSP), or one of the more traditional methodologies dicussed in Chapter 4, for example SSADM. While this is an open activity, you will find further discussion of this activity on the Web site which accompanies this book.

Further reading

There is a range of further reading that we can recommend in this area, all of which aim to stimulate you into thinking why a particular process or methodology may be more or less appropriate, or looking to find alternative ways to make such an assessment.

As an alternative framework to the CMM, you might like to consider the following as a means of comparing and evaluating methodologies:

> Jayaratna, N., *Understanding and Evaluating Methodologies: NIMSAD – A Systemic Framework,* McGraw Hill, 1999, ISBN 0-07-707882-9

For further examples of using the CMM to compare methodologies you could consult the following white paper. This was the original paper that inspired us to consider using the CMM as a means to compare methodologies and we consider it a particularly good read:

> Ambler, S.W., *Enterprise Unified Process: Enhancing the Unified Process to Meet the Real-World Needs of Your Organisation,* Ronin International Inc, Oct 1999, (posted at www.sdmagazine.com)

The following is an interesting white paper publication from Rational, which makes reference to applying the RUP to support an organisation's progression through the CMM maturity levels.

> *Reaching CMM Levels 2 and 3 with the Rational Unified Process,* a Rational Software White Paper,

For references on the RUP, Catalysis and XP please refer to the *Further reading* section in Chapter 4. General references on the CMM can be found in the *Further reading* section in Chapter 10.

Appendices

Appendix A

UML Notation

This appendix gives a concise summary of the key parts of the UML notation. It is divided into two main sections. Section 1 covers the core modelling notation, by a series of annotated examples. It is structured primarily according to diagram type. Section 2 deals with extension mechanisms and the OCL, which we have termed advanced features.

A.1   Core modelling notation

A.1.1 Use case diagrams

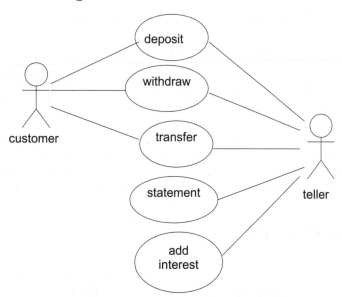

Figure A.1: Simple use case diagram

A simple use case diagram, such as figure A.1, contains three types of model element. Actors are shown as stick people, use cases are ovals and the associations, indicating participation, between actors and use cases are shown as lines.

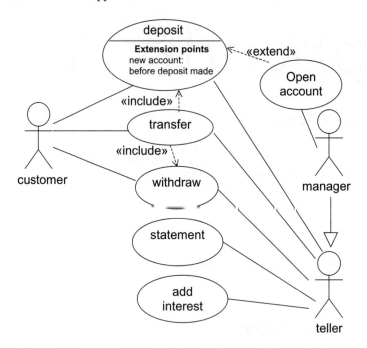

Figure A.2: More sophisticated use case diagram

Figure A.2 shows a more sophisticated use of the notation.

The use of inheritance to describe associations between actors can add useful clarity. The generalised actor, **manager** here, has all the same roles as the generalisation, but can perform some additional activities.

Dependencies between use cases can be shown, and are typically adorned with the stereotype «include» or «extend». A use case which includes another copies the other's behaviour as part of its description at some point. A use case which extends another adds its behaviour to that of the other at an extension point. A use case can also specialise another.

A.1.2 Class diagrams

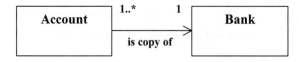

A.3: Association and multiplicities

Elements of class diagrams include

- rectangles with names
    - classes
    - signals
    - other classifiers
- lines joining classes
    - associations
- labels on lines
    - names of associations
- numbers or ranges on ends of lines
    - multiplicities of association roles
- solid black triangles
    - indicate direction of association when ambiguous
- Navigability
    - Open arrow heads on the associations show navigability
    - This indicates which object needs to know about which other object to make an association work
    - Where no navigability is shown this can mean two way or not yet defined. Be consistent

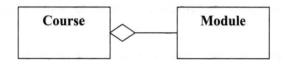

A.4: Aggregation

Aggregation, shown in figure A.4, is a tighter form of association, where one class, the one with the diamond at its end, has the other as a part of itself. The part can, however, be deleted or replaced without its owner being destroyed.

A.5: Composition

Composition, shown in figure A.5, is a tighter form of association still, where one class, the one with the black diamond at its end, has the other as an integral part of itself. The part cannot, now, be deleted or replaced without its owner being destroyed.

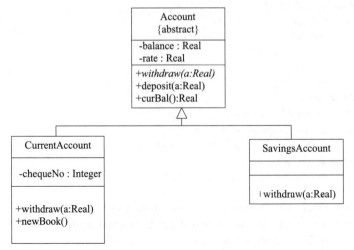

A.6: Generalisation and specialisation

Figure A.6 shows the use of specialisation (or generalisation if you prefer). Account fully defines the operations **deposit()** and **curBal()**. These are not re-defined in **CurrentAccount** or **SavingsAccount**.

Operation **withdraw()** is not implemented at the level of **Account**. This makes **Account** an abstract class, shown by the property **{abstract}** below its name. You cannot have meaningful objects based just on an abstract class.

SavingsAccount is a specialisation of Account and contains the implementation of withdraw(). This matches the one required for any type of Account, which was shown in italics in **Account**. This means that we can generate objects (instances) of **SavingsAccount**.

CurrentAccount also defines its own version of **withdraw()**. **CurrentAccount** also adds some new attributes and operations to support the use of cheque books. A specialisation may also redefine operations which were implemented in its parent.

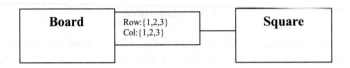

A.7: Qualified association

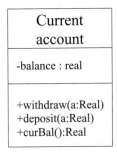

A8: Class with internal details shown

Figure A.8 shows a class with its standard internal details exposed. A class can be divided into three or more compartments. The standard three need not be labelled. Others should have a clear label, indicating what the list they hold contains.

The standard three compartments are:
- Name at the top
- Attributes in the middle
  - protection +, # or -   public, protected or private
  - label : type
- Operations at the bottom
  - protection +, # or -   public, protected or private
  - label(parameters)   parameter is label:type or just type
  - : type   optional return type

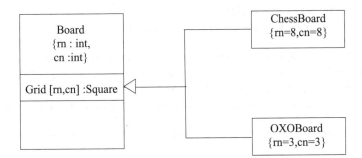

A9: Class diagram with properties

Figure A9 shows the use of properties of classes. A property to restrict the way a class may be used, most commonly to define {abstract} classes. We can also specify almost any other properties we might find useful. One important use of this is to define initial values for attributes of a class. We can also define invariant properties.

In fact properties may be used in many places in UML, including after attributes, but their use in classes is the most common

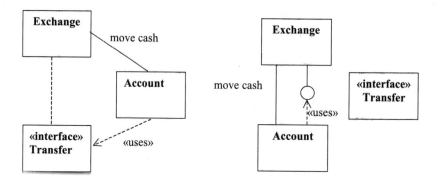

A.10: Alternative forms for presenting interfaces

Figure A.10 shows the use of interfaces. Since, when following the principle of encapsulation, we are only allowed to see the operations of a class, two classes with the same operations should be interchangeable. This gives us the most abstract view of an object – its *interface*. If someone else is developing the class from which some of our objects are derived, all we have is the interface. We can still build our part of the system. The interface is like a completely abstract class.

The two versions of interface notation are equivalent.
- The "lollipop" symbol is more convenient if the interface is already defined.
- The association (move cash) is between the class using the interface and the class supporting it.
- The «uses» link is a dependency.
- The implementation link is a sort of specialisation.

Figure A.11 shows the use of packages to represent the importing of elements from a library (package) into another package which will use these elements. This example is based on a student exercise, where the UML diagram was used to provide a specification of the system students had to build, using various standard elements from Java's AWT library.

Note the use of stereotyped dependencies from the package being built to those being imported.

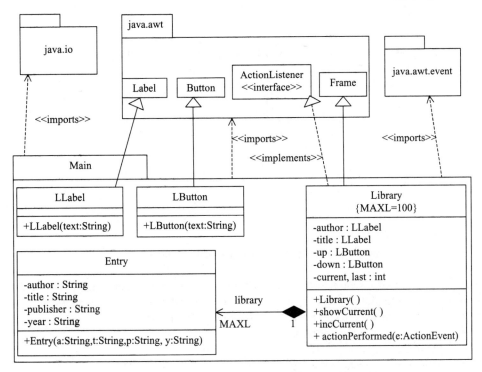

Figure A.11: Use of packages with class diagrams

A.1.3 Interactions

UML provides two sorts of interaction diagram. Sequence diagrams show sequences of messages with the emphasis on the order in which they are sent. Collaboration diagrams show how systems are built from objects and how messages get sent. A sequence diagram shows the behaviour of a collection of interacting objects (see example in figure A.11):

- The objects are drawn at the top (or left)
- Each has a dashed *lifeline* going down (or rightwards) showing the order of events for it
- Messages are sent leaving one object's lifeline and reaching another's
- The times when an object is busy can be shown by overlaying thin rectangles called *activations*
- Object names have an optional label, a colon then the class that the object belongs to, all underlined

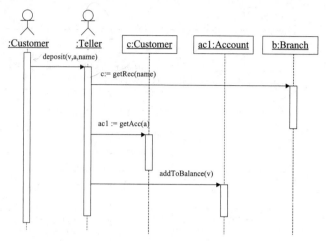

Figure A.12: Example sequence diagram

Figure A.13 provides a reminder about key notations of interaction diagrams, in particular the message and signal types supported by both sequence and collaboration diagrams.

- Shown as arrows – with requests for operations for messages
- May be (nestedly) numbered
- Parameters may be passed
- Values may be returned using assignment :=
- Sub-sequences may be enclosed in a box
- Messages or sub-sequences may be conditional on a guard in square brackets
- Messages or sub-sequences may be repeated – shown by *, with messages boxed if necessary to reflect repeated grouping

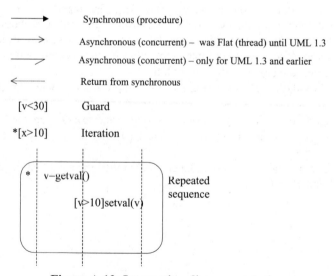

Figure A.13: Interaction diagram notation

A collaboration is a collection of instances or objects which are associated with each other (see example in figure A.14):

- The classes from which the objects are derived must have associations
- There may be multiple instances of any class present
- Only those associations relevant to the current scenario need to be shown
- Objects are shown as rectangles
- Each object has a colon followed by the class of the object
- An instance name may be specified before the colon
- The names are usually underlined for clarity
- Actors (instances of actors) may be used as well as objects

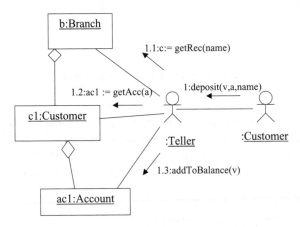

Figure A.14: Example collaboration diagram

Message numbering is a way of defining order. This is particularly important for collaboration diagrams (though the extra clarity can also help on sequence diagrams too):

- Procedural (synchronous) messages are ordered in a nested way to show cause and effect   (as shown in figure A.14)

1	1.1	1.1.1	etc.

- Parallel or concurrent sequences are independent of each other. They form partial orderings. 1.1.1a and 1.1.1b represent the start of concurrent partial orders

1.1.1a.1	1.1.1a.2	etc.
1.1.1b.1	1.1.1b.2	etc

A.1.4 Statecharts

The following is a reminder of key notation for statecharts, as shown in figure A.15.

- States are shown as lozenges (rectangles with rounded corners)
- Each state has a name, which should be meaningful
- Transitions are shown as arrows linking states
- A transition usually has a trigger written next to it

- Triggers are usually incoming messages

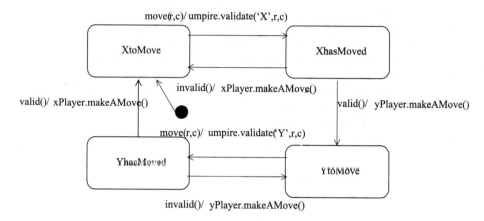

Figure A.15: Example statechart

Messages and signals:
- The messages (and signals) in statecharts are of the same form as in interactions
- A message may have parameters, e.g. **move(r,c)**
- A message may generate a value, e.g. **isValid:=validate('X',r,c)**
- A signal is a special communication between objects and looks just like a message

Actions on transitions (shown in figure A.15):
- Once triggered, a transition is said to fire
- A transition may cause actions as part of its firing
- Some actions are changes to local or global variables
  - **count++**
- Some are output actions, sending messages or signals
  - **umpire.validate('X',r,c)**
- A sequence of actions can be used, separated by ; or some other separator symbol

Special states:
- A circle with a smaller black circle at its centre is an end state (shown on figures A.16 and A.17)
- A black filled circle is a start state (shown on figures A.15 to A.17)
- All statecharts should have a start state
- A state can represent an activity, not just waiting
- A state can be made up of several sub-states (shown later in figure A.17)

Further examples of triggers are shown in figure A.16.
- A transition can be triggered by the passage of time
  - **after(10secs)**

- A transition can be triggered by a condition becoming true
  - ○ **when(tries=6)**
- A transition can be triggered implicitly by the completion of the internal activity of a state
- A trigger can be guarded by a condition; the condition is tested after the trigger
  - ○ **ask(m) [tries<6]**

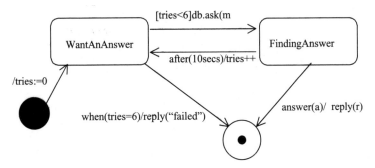

Figure A.16: Guards and iteration

Nested and super states (shown in figure A.17); we follow the rules listed, not all of which are enforced by the UML definition:

- A super state is one containing an internal state machine
- The internal state machine must have a start state and an end state
- The transitions arriving at a super state all go to the internal start state
- The transitions leaving a super state all come from its internal end state

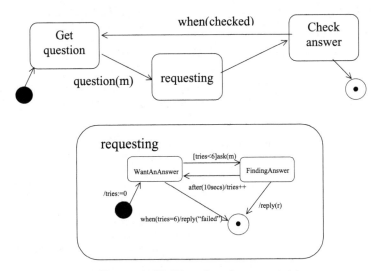

Figure A.17: Nested and super states

As well as labelling transitions with actions, it is possible to define actions within a state (refer to example in figure A.18). This form should not be mixed with super state/sub-state notation.

- **entry** – defines an action to be performed on entering a state
- **exit** – defines an action to be performed when leaving a state
- **do** – defines an action to be performed while in a state

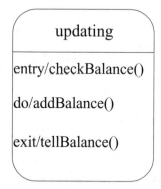

updating

entry/checkBalance()

do/addBalance()

exit/tellBalance()

Figure A.18: Exit, entry and do actions within a state

A.1.5 Activity diagrams

Activity diagrams have notation in common with statecharts. A summary of key notation is provided in table A.1.

Modelling icon	Name	UML Definition
→	Transition	Arrow indicating movement between actions
(rounded rectangle)	Activity	An activity used on activity diagram
● ◉	Start State End State	These symbols show the start and end states on activity diagrams and statecharts
▬	Synchronisation Bar	Used to split and synchronise paths between activities (also used on statecharts)
◇	Decision	Decision points between activities (can also used on statecharts)
[t<10]	Guard	As used on statechart, the guard is used to represent some condition which must be true for the transition to fire. It is tested after the trigger, if any.

Table A.1: Action diagram notation

- Swimlanes can be used to partition behaviour on any basis we wish (see example in figure A.19)
- Some synchronisations can be better shown as the need for one stream of activity to share an object with another
- In particular, one activity may be shown as creating an object which is needed by another. This similar to dataflow – in business terms this is workflow (see figure A.19)

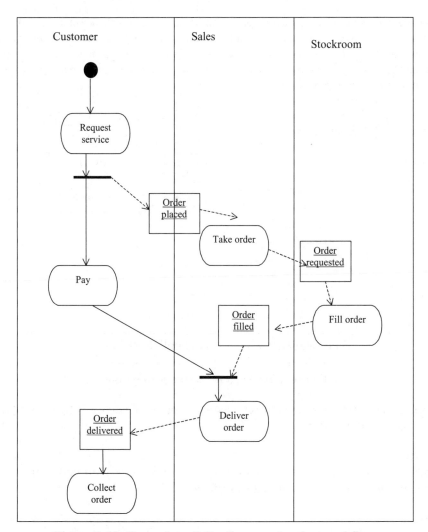

Figure A.19: Example activity diagram showing workflow

A.1.6 Package notation

Packages are used to hold collections of model elements. In general there is no restriction on what can be collected together in a package. Packages can be used to restrict access to their elements rather like a class can restrict access. Elements within a package are owned by that package, and can be imported or accessed by other packages. Packages can belong to enclosing packages. A simple package diagram for classes was shown in figure A.11.

A package with none of its elements shown can be drawn as a tabbed rectangle with a label in the larger rectangle. A package with all or some of its contents shown inside the larger rectangle has its label on the tab. An alternative is to show elements attached by a ⊕ headed line from the owning package to the owned elements shown outside the package. Examples of these are shown in figure A.20.

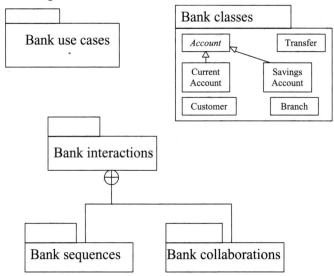

Figure A.20: Example package diagrams

Elements in other packages can be either imported or accessed (shown in figure A.21 taken from the OMG specification):

«import»
- adds the elements in the imported package to the name space of the importing package
- removes the need to use a pathname to refer to these

«access»
- merely allows references to the elements in the accessed package
- to set up a reference the package pathname must be used

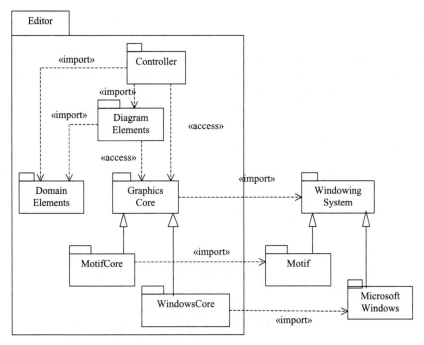

Figure A.21: Using package elements

A.1.7 Component and deployment diagrams

Nodes:
- The diagram in figure A.22 shows just the hardware of a system
- The nodes are devices such as PCs and workstations
- The links are association instances representing how these devices communicate to send messages

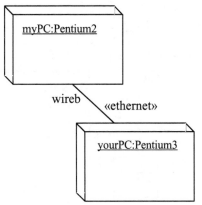

Figure A.22: Node diagram

Components:
- Components represent pieces of software
- They are related by dependencies
- In figure A.23 we show the compile time dependencies which are used in making files and project files (showing compile time components)

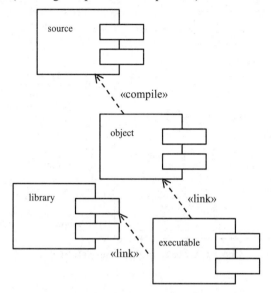

Figure A.23: Compile time components

Runtime dependencies are perhaps more useful:
- These show how types of component rely on each other to function (see figure A.24)
- Runtime components may have interfaces or be unadorned

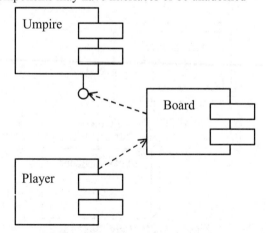

Figure A.24: Runtime components

Deployment diagrams:
- By combining the node and component information, we can see how components are deployed (see figure A.25)
- All dependencies between components must be matched by a means of sending message
- procedure calling on the same node
- physical communications link between nodes
- The deployment shown seems to overload myPC

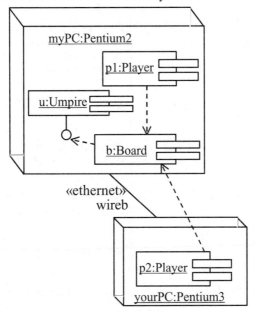

Figure A.25: Deployment diagram

A.1.8 Business modelling

The value of using UML for business modelling is to reuse an established notation (i.e. UML) to provide a common language and potentially a common tool (a UML visual modelling CASE tool) for all modelling needs. This section focusses on the UML and its support for business modelling.

Table A.1 describes the notation which has a business specific icon (as supported by Rational Rose). These business specific icons have similar non-business counterparts (e.g. there is a Business Actor icon and an Actor icon, a Business Use Case icon and Use Case icon). The intention in providing business specific notation is that this distinction in visual icons can help clarify a business element from a different unit.

Modelling icon	**Name**	**UML Definition**
	Business actor	Someone or something, outside the business that interacts with the business
	Business worker	Role or set of roles inside the business. A business worker interacts with other business workers and manipulates business entities
	Business entity	A "thing" handled or used by business workers
	Business use case	A sequence of actions a business performs that yields an observable result of value to a particular business actor. (In this paper, synonymous with business process)
	Activity	An activity used on activity diagram
	Start State End State	These symbols show the start and end states on activity diagrams and statecharts
	Synchronisation Bar	Used to split and synchronise paths between activities (also used on statecharts)
	Decision	Decision points between activities (also used on statecharts)

Table A.2: Core business modelling notation

Additional extensions to UML have been proposed to support business modelling. The Eriksson-Penker Business Extensions adapt the basic UML activity diagram and introduce what they refer to as the *process diagram*. An illustration of key notations from the proposed extension is shown in table A.2.

Modelling icon	Name	UML Definition
«text here»	Stereotype	Text shown in chevron brackets which is used for extra clarification.
«process» Name	Business process	A process, takes input resources from its left-hand side and indicates its output resources on its right-hand side (shown as dependencies to and from the process, according to standard UML syntax). The process symbol may also include the stereotype «process» for extra clarification. The Name is a textual description of the process.
Name	Business object	An object which is input to or output from an object. A stereotype may be added to clarify, for example to reflects process goals («goal»), physical resource («resource»), or people («people»). The Name is a textual description of the object.
«information» Name	Information object	An object, which is specifically identified as information. The alternative icon is used for clarity.
--------->	Dependency	Connecting line with arrow shows dependencies between model components. Direction of arrow indicates direction of dependency. This can also be annotated with a stereotype to clarify the nature of dependency.

Table A.3: Additional proposed extensions

A.2   Advanced notation

A.2.1 Defining stereotypes

Stereotypes are the most common mechanism that you may have already seen. Stereotypes are included in the double chevron braces, for example «uses» or «extends» and «interface». A number of stereotypes are already defined in the UML language, but modellers can define additional ones as required. A stereotype defines a more specialised form of a basic element of UML. Both **class** and **actor** are, thus, stereotypes of the basic element type, **classifier**. In the case of **actor**, a new icon is used, which is an alternative way of showing a stereotype within the notation.

Tag definitions comprise both a tag's name and its type. They are used to add named attributes to an existing UML element type when a stereotype is defined. Tagged values can then be used to specify a constraint on either a stereotype or an instance of an element, including a stereotype.

Constraints are provided as a mechanism that defines limits (i.e. constraints) on a model element, especially its tags and attributes. These may be defined using free format text, or more formally using the Object Constraint Language (OCL). Constraints are enclosed in curly braces, for example {amount is multiple of £10.00} may be a constraint against an attribute or a tag in a class.

FigureA.26 shows the definition of a new stereotype, Persistent, which is a specialisation of Class, using tag definitions and constraints. Any instance of Persistent will have to give values to these tags, while respecting the constraint.

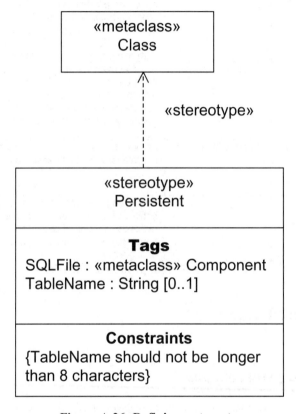

Figure A.26: Defining a stereotype

Further reading

Eriksson, H.-E. and Penker, M. (2000) *Business Modelling with UML: Business Patterns at Work*, John Wiley & Sons, New York.

Business Modelling with the UML and Rational Suite AnalystStudio, Rational whitepaper, http://www.rational.com/products/whitepapers/102017.jsp

Appendix B
The Importance of Tool Support

Throughout most of this book we have advocated the use of UML as a paper and pencil exercise. This does not mean that computer-based tools don't have a part to play – but they are no substitute in themselves for good modelling skills. Our experience of people learning UML is that tools can often hinder their progress because it is too easy to become distracted by the way the tool works rather than thinking in a more open way about what it is that you are trying to achieve.

Tools do have an important role in supporting modelling activities, but it is worth identifying in what way we expect the tool to support us. This is similar to the argument we have made in this book about the use of appropriate processes/methodologies. We can easily agree that the use of tools and methodologies are good in principle, but when we get right down to it what exactly is it that they provide us with which makes one or other a better choice?

Think for a moment what it is that you expect a tool to do for you. Is it just about drawing diagrams and improving the quality and clarity of the diagrams being drawn, as opposed to their hand drawn counterparts? If so, then a UML modelling tool is not the only option. Consider the diagrams in this book. Certain of these were produced using Rational Rose, certain using argoUML, others were drawn directly using Microsoft Word, and others again were scanned images of hand drawn diagrams. The latter are the easiest to spot in the text, and the others you may be able to spot if you are familiar with one or more of the drawing capabilities of the tools mentioned. Diagrams produced using a particular UML modelling tool tend to have a certain appearance, often most notable where use case diagrams are concerned – the actors and use cases tend to appear slightly different in different tools.

There may often be more to it than just drawing diagrams. Do you want the tool to act as a reminder or checker of the notation that you are using? This can be helpful if you are not entirely familiar with the subset of UML that you are using. How important is it to use correct or precise UML notation? If you want to use any model checking utilities (which certain tools offer) or you want to use code generation utilities, then it can be particularly important.

In this appendix we expand on the above points and offer a summary of benefits and criteria that you might like to consider when looking at tool support for your own modelling activities. We also explore further the issues of code generation and reverse engineering, as these are increasingly desirable areas that necessitate tool support.

Benefits of tool support

In this section we consider a number of benefits of using tools to support UML modelling activities. It can take a significant amount of time to draw and document a model using any tool. It is important to think what added value this activity provides – what is the value of using the tool? It certainly provides a repository of model information, which can be important in itself, but in what ways do you intend to use the model? Who else needs to access it (through the same or different tool, or through some form of dissemination of model information) and are there any additional intentions, such as to generate code from the model? The following are some key points to consider in choosing a tool. Consider how many of these apply to you and then look for a tool (or tools) that can provide you with that.

Drawing capabilities	Layout, consistency of style
Diagram support	What UML diagram support do you actually require? Think about the range of UML diagrams that you might typically want to use and examine how well a given tool supports that diagram. Avoid assuming that each tool that purports to support UML will do so in an equivocal way. Some are better at particular diagrams than others. Draw yourself up a separate checklist of UML that is immediately important to your work, i.e. use case, class, activity, sequence, collaboration, state and package. What about support for OCL, workflow, business modelling notation and any profiles of interest to your domain?
Documentation	What capabilities are provided for supporting documentation related to a diagram? Can you record documentation at the diagram and/or component level (e.g. individual use case, classifier, activity etc.)
Report generation	What reports can the tool provide based on diagrams and recorded documentation?
Model analysis/ checking/ validation	Related to reports, there may be additional analysis which would support model checking. This may be in the form of checking that objects on dynamic diagrams (interaction, state, activity) are based on classes identified on a class diagram. Certain metric/statistical information may also be available through the tool, for example class
Model interchange (export/import)	You may want to move the model between different installations of tool, or share with other people using different tools. What export options/formats are supported?
Web publishing	Web publishing can be a beneficial means to disseminate/share model information. If you are unfamiliar with this then you might like to look at the case study in Chapter 8.
Diagram extraction	Is there any easy means to extract/export diagram images to use in other media (e.g. reports or documentation that the tool itself does not support). Think about how you might want to use the images themselves.

Extras   Some tools provide added value/flexibility in drawing diagrams. For example the ability to use non-standard component sizes (resizing components such as use cases or classes). Some tools provide support in layout. Further still, some tools support automatic conversion between certain diagrams (most notably between collaboration and sequence diagrams). What extras might you be looking for, or what are offered by particular tools?

Other utilities, such as supporting the drawing of composite diagrams, are not well supported by UML tools. These diagrams can be helpful at times, for example see figures 6.9 in Chapter 6 and figure 8.2 in Chapter 8. For such diagrams we advise that you use the more flexible drawing capabilities of tools such as MS Word, Visio or any other general drawing tool with which you are familiar.

In addition to the above criteria, the following are some additional practical issues to consider:

Cost   This can often be an overriding factor, as tools tend to be expensive. This is another good reason to consider the real reasons in wanting to use a tool as discussed above. Having the most expensive and comprehensive tool does not make for a better modelling job in itself.

Flexibility/ Portability   Does the tool need to run in different environments, across different platforms. Do you need to support remote working, either standalone (e.g. laptop) or via the Internet?

Support   How much support do you require from the supplying company – consider the level of support they offer and how beneficial that may be (training, documentation, helpline etc.)

Upgrade   What is the supplier upgrade policy/arrangement? Given the fact that the UML is a moving standard, how important is it that your tool stays current. This will depend more on whether you require the tool to support OCL and/or any developing UML profiles. Again we would argue that many people can work adequately with the core UML notation discussed in this book. Technologies to support model interchange are important, and another area in which upgrades may become important.

Stability   How established is the drawing package/tool – does it have a proven track record?

Working Practices   Are there existing working practices to be supported? For example, group modelling activities can be increasingly supported via tools such as the interactive whiteboard technologies.

Code generation and reverse engineering

Code generation and reverse engineering are both common reasons people cite as benefits of using a modelling tool. In this section we discuss what code generation and round trip engineering are, and their relevance to you as a UML practitioner.

Code generation is about producing code directly from a recorded model. This is one of the benefits and motivations for having a standard modelling notation. In the simplest sense we are talking about producing skeleton object-oriented code from static model information available from the class diagram. Information from the class diagram supports production of a class outline, with attributes specified with type and access level. Skeleton code can also be provided which specifies method signatures. This leaves a deal of program logic to be implemented by the software developer. As basic as this sounds, this is still a helpful contribution as it provides consistency between the model and the code implementation. Increasingly sophisticated code generation is becoming possible by taking additional logic details from the dynamic UML diagrams, for example interaction diagrams.

Reverse engineering concerns the opposite of code generation. Here we assume that we are taking source code and producing a model of that code. As with code generation, the obvious connection to be made is in extracting class details which helps to identify the code structure and specify associated attributes and operations.

We can take both ideas of reverse engineering and code generation and combine them to consider round trip engineering. Consider a situation where we have software which has been in use for some time and is not entirely well understood. The world is full of a great deal of code that fits this description, and it occurs for a wide variety of reasons. This might be because, while there was a model of the system at some point, modifications to the code over recent months/years mean that we are no longer certain that the code matches the original model. We could reverse engineer the code and begin to understand its purpose and operation through the resulting model. The model may be modified/adapted and then a code generation utility applied to generate a new revised version of the application. This cyclic process can be repeated and ensures that periodically we synchronise both model and code implementation.

Further references

Since the subject of modelling tools varies quickly we have decided to limit ourselves to putting further information on this subject on the Web site which accompanies this textbook (refer to the Preface for further information). We hope that you will find consulting that additional information and selected links there of interest.

Index